POEMS FOR HAPPINESS

More poetry available from
Macmillan Collector's Library

Poems for Little Ones introduced by Michael Morpurgo

Poems for Travellers introduced by Paul Theroux

Poems on Nature introduced by Helen Macdonald

Poems for Christmas introduced by Judith Flanders

Poems for Love introduced by Joanna Trollope

Poems to Swipe Right To ed. Charlie Castelletti

The Golden Treasury ed. Francis Turner Palgrave

A Golden Treasury of Irish Verse ed. Lennox Robinson

Leaves of Grass: Selected Poems by Walt Whitman

Selected Poems by John Keats

Collected Poems by W. B. Yeats

The Sonnets by William Shakespeare

Poetry of the First World War ed. Marcus Clapham

Tales and Poems by Edgar Allan Poe

The Rime of the Ancient Mariner by Samuel Taylor Coleridge

POEMS FOR HAPPINESS

With an introduction by
RICHARD COLES

Selection and arrangement by
GABY MORGAN

MACMILLAN COLLECTOR'S LIBRARY

This collection first published 2019 by Macmillan Collector's Library

This edition published 2026 by Macmillan Collector's Library
an imprint of Pan Macmillan
The Smithson, 6 Briset Street, London EC1M 5NR
EU representative: Macmillan Publishers Ireland Ltd, 1st Floor,
The Liffey Trust Centre, 117–126 Sheriff Street Upper,
Dublin 1 D01 YC43
Associated companies throughout the world

ISBN 978-1-0350-6307-9

Selection and arrangement copyright © Gaby Morgan 2019
Introduction copyright © The Reverend Richard Coles 2019

Scripture quotations from The Authorized (King James) Version. Rights in the Authorized Version in the United Kingdom are vested in the Crown. Reproduced by permission of the Crown's patentee, Cambridge University Press

All rights reserved. No part of this publication may be reproduced, stored in a retrieval system, or transmitted, in any form, or by any means (including, without limitation, electronic, mechanical, photocopying, recording or otherwise) without the prior written permission of the publisher.

1 3 5 7 9 8 6 4 2

A CIP catalogue record for this book is available from the British Library.

Cover and endpaper design: Daisy Bates, Pan Macmillan Art Department

Typeset by Six Red Marbles UK, Thetford, Norfolk
Printed and bound in China by Imago

This book is sold subject to the condition that it shall not, by way of trade or otherwise, be lent, hired out, or otherwise circulated without the publisher's prior consent in any form of binding or cover other than that in which it is published and without a similar condition including this condition being imposed on the subsequent purchaser. The publisher does not authorize the use or reproduction of any part of this book in any manner for the purpose of training artificial intelligence technologies or systems. The publisher expressly reserves this book from the Text and Data Mining exception in accordance with Article 4(3) of the European Union Digital Single Market Directive 2019/790.

Visit **www.panmacmillan.com** to read more
about all our books and to buy them.

Contents

Introduction xiii

HAPPY THOUGHT

Happy Thought *Robert Louis Stevenson* 3

Happy the Man *John Dryden* 4

New Sights *Anon.* 5

On a Quiet Conscience *Charles I* 6

Leisure *W. H. Davies* 7

High Flight *John Gillespie Magee Jr* 8

May the Road Rise Up to Meet You *Anon.* 9

If *Rudyard Kipling* 10

Now May Every Living Thing *Anon.* 12

Hurt No Living Thing *Christina Rossetti* 13

from Auguries of Innocence *William Blake* 14

To Every Thing There Is a Season
Book of Ecclesiastes 15

from Endymion *John Keats* 16

Shining Things *Elizabeth Gould* 17

The Quiet Life *Alexander Pope* 19

Song of Apollo *Percy Bysshe Shelley* 20

My Mind to Me a Kingdom Is *Sir Edward Dyer* 22

On First Looking into Chapman's Homer
John Keats 24

Contents

Eternity *William Blake* 25

A Farewell *Charles Kingsley* 26

A Vision *Henry Vaughan* 27

Gratefulnesse *George Herbert* 28

Thanks in Old Age *Walt Whitman* 30

A Little Health *Anon.* 31

GLORY BE TO GOD FOR DAPPLED THINGS

Pied Beauty *Gerard Manley Hopkins* 35

Amazing Grace *John Newton* 36

God Be In My Head *Sarum Missal* 37

'Lord, make me an instrument of Thy peace'
St Francis of Assisi 38

Miracles *Walt Whitman* 39

Father, We Thank Thee *Ralph Waldo Emerson* 40

African Canticle *Anon.* 41

The Thanksgivings *Iroquois, Traditional
tr. Harriet Maxwell Converse* 42

Harvest Home *Henry Alford* 44

Swing Low, Sweet Chariot *Wallace Willis* 46

Desiderata *Max Ehrmann* 47

The Iroquois Prayer *Iroquois, Traditional* 49

Jewish Prayer *Service of the Orthodox
Synagogue for the Festival of Tabernacles* 50

from His Pilgrimage *Sir Walter Raleigh* 51

Contents

When the Heart is Hard *Rabindranath Tagore* 52

The Selkirk Grace *Robert Burns* 53

Epitaph *Winifred Holtby* 54

I SING OF BROOKS, OF BLOSSOMS, BIRDS, AND BOWERS

The Argument of His Book *Robert Herrick* 57

The Song of Wandering Aengus *W. B. Yeats* 58

Spring *William Blake* 59

I Wandered Lonely as a Cloud *William Wordsworth* 60

I'll Tell You How the Sun Rose *Emily Dickinson* 61

The Happy Child *W. H. Davies* 62

from Pippa Passes *Robert Browning* 63

A Greeting *W. H. Davies* 64

February Twilight *Sara Teasdale* 65

Adoration *Christopher Smart* 66

The Sun Rising *John Donne* 67

Sowing *Edward Thomas* 69

A Dumb Friend *Christina Rossetti* 70

My Heart Leaps Up *William Wordsworth* 72

The Throstle *Alfred, Lord Tennyson* 73

May *Thomas Dekker* 74

Moonlight, Summer Moonlight *Emily Brontë* 75

The Lake Isle of Innisfree *W. B. Yeats* 76

Contents

Where the Bee Sucks *William Shakespeare* 77

To Make a Prairie *Emily Dickinson* 78

from A Midsummer Night's Dream
William Shakespeare 79

Careless Rambles *John Clare* 80

Magna Est Veritas *Coventry Patmore* 81

Rest and Be Thankful! *William Wordsworth* 82

Composed Upon Westminster Bridge, September 3,
1802 *William Wordsworth* 83

Moonlit Apples *John Drinkwater* 84

Harvest Hymn *John Greenleaf Whittier* 85

To Autumn *John Keats* 86

Pleasant Sounds *John Clare* 88

'See yonder leafless trees against the sky'
Ralph Waldo Emerson 89

Evening Quatrains *Charles Cotton* 90

Ode *Joseph Addison* 92

'It is a beauteous evening, calm and free'
William Wordsworth 93

God's Grandeur *Gerard Manley Hopkins* 94

SAY NOT THE STRUGGLE
NOUGHT AVAILETH

Say Not the Struggle Nought Availeth
Arthur Hugh Clough 97

Freedom *Olive Runner* 98

Contents

New Every Morning *Susan Coolidge* 99

Will *Ella Wheeler Wilcox* 100

Invictus *W. E. Henley* 101

Ain't I a Woman? *Sojourner Truth and Erlene Stetson* 102

This, Too, Shall Pass Away *Lanta Wilson Smith* 104

'Hope' is the Thing with Feathers *Emily Dickinson* 105

Shut Not Your Doors to Me, Proud Libraries *Walt Whitman* 106

Courage *Amelia Earhart* 107

The Call *Charlotte Mew* 108

A Pebble *James W. Foley* 109

from Henry V *William Shakespeare* 111

The New Colossus *Emma Lazarus* 112

The Gettysburg Address *Abraham Lincoln* 113

The Star-Spangled Banner *Francis Scott Key* 114

I Hear America Singing *Walt Whitman* 116

No Coward Soul Is Mine *Emily Brontë* 117

A Summing Up *Charles Mackay* 119

FRIENDSHIP IS LOVE
WITHOUT HIS WINGS

L'Amitié Est L'Amour Sans Ailes *Lord Byron* 123

Outwitted *Edwin Markham* 126

We Two Boys Together Clinging *Walt Whitman* 127

Contents

Friendship *Dinah Maria Craik*   128

Forbearance *Ralph Waldo Emerson*   129

Friendship *Aztec, Traditional*   130

Travelling *William Wordsworth*   131

Love and Friendship *Emily Brontë*   132

New Friends and Old Friends *Joseph Parry*   133

HE WISHES FOR THE CLOTHS OF HEAVEN

He Wishes for the Cloths of Heaven *W. B. Yeats*   137

How Do I Love Thee? *Elizabeth Barrett Browning*   138

Sonnet 18 *William Shakespeare*   139

Meeting at Night *Robert Browning*   140

To a Friend *Amy Lowell*   141

A Birthday *Christina Rossetti*   142

Upon Julia's Clothes *Robert Herrick*   143

Rose-cheeked Laura *Thomas Campion*   144

In an Artist's Studio *Christina Rossetti*   145

'It was a lover and his lass' *William Shakespeare*   146

Love Lightly Pleased *Robert Herrick*   147

Invitation to Love *Paul Laurence Dunbar*   148

from Paradise Lost *John Milton*   149

Fulfillment *William Cavendish*   150

from Sonnets from the Portuguese *Elizabeth Barrett Browning*   151

x

Contents

Camomile Tea *Katherine Mansfield* 152

When I Heard at the Close of the Day
Walt Whitman 153

Song *George Peele* 154

To Althea, from Prison *Richard Lovelace* 155

A Decade *Amy Lowell* 157

THE SHAPE OF A GOOD GREYHOUND

The Shape of a Good Greyhound *Anon.* 161

The Lurcher *William Cowper* 162

Dog *Harold Monro* 163

The Windhover *Gerard Manley Hopkins* 165

A Winter Bluejay *Sara Teasdale* 166

from To a Skylark *Percy Bysshe Shelley* 167

'Pack, clouds, away, and welcome day'
Thomas Heywood 168

from Jubilate Agno *Christopher Smart* 169

Pangur Bán *Anon. tr. Robin Flower* 173

The Owl and the Pussycat *Edward Lear* 175

Seal Lullaby *Rudyard Kipling* 177

Index of Poets 179

Index of Titles 183

Index of First Lines 189

Introduction

RICHARD COLES

Happiness writes white, observed Montherlant, meaning I suppose that it is the drama of weal and woe that excites and captivates us rather than happiness, a state of contentment that is cloudless, bland even. You can see this difficulty in Botticelli's illustrations for Dante's *Divine Comedy*, drawn in the fifteenth century. The pilgrim's progress through Hell and Purgatory is vividly shown, each circle of Hell as busy and complex as Piccadilly Circus; by the time he has stepped into Paradise, however, it all gets a bit abstract, and in the end he and his guide, Virgil, float around geometric shapes as they enter a perfect state of bliss.

Floating ecstatically around a giant circle is all very well, but I think there is more to say about happiness than that. Happiness, even if white, is not just white: it is off-white, ivory, cream, kid, glacier, imperial ermine – and you need only glance at the colour chart for a posh paint company to see how inventive one has to be to capture its range.

These poems are, then, Fifty Shades of White. They explore the range of the human experience of happiness: as a passing moment that vanishes the second one settles on it; as the reward for luck and good choices; as the steady contentment which the truly fortunate may find.

For the first category poetry is especially apt, for nothing captures so delicately, and perhaps fatally, the passing moment. Gerard Manley Hopkins's 'Pied

Introduction

Beauty' is one of my favourites, not least because the poet is associated with my parish at Finedon. The love of his life – in this world – was Digby Dolben, son of its squire, an extraordinarily eccentric youth so easily bored that he did away with the necessity of visiting a barber when he was at Eton by singeing off his surplus locks with a candle. He was a precociously gifted boy too, leaving a collection of verse which is as surprisingly vivid as it is arch. He was also a religious maniac, affected the name Brother Laurence and wandered the parish in a Benedictine habit until, aged nineteen, he drowned playing with his tutor's son in the River Welland. I digress. But there is something mercurial about Dolben which Hopkins captured in this breathtaking poem in praise of kaleidoscopic variety, those shifts of surface and light that flash unexpectedly and illuminate. When I read this I recall a period of intense happiness in my own life, the summer of 1990 on the island of Ibiza, when the memories that are still intelligible are precisely that, flashes of light from the glittering sea, strobe-frozen tableaux from Amnesia and Ku, and the party people, ragtag and bobtail, hurled together by ecstasy, House and the energy of being young. For Hopkins, that pied beauty is not only the play of light and reflection, nor perhaps over-stimulated synapses on a party isle in the second summer of love, but also the knotty particularities of a trade, a calling, a proficiency, which angle those skilled in them to the mainstream. It is a very peculiar juxtaposition, the stipple on a trout and a plough horse's bridle – what could be more different? – yet for Hopkins they both speak of the glory of God: various, unexpected, textured.

For Hopkins, in the end, that dazzling and surprising

Introduction

variety is the creativity of God breaking forth in the world; others have no need of such a hypothesis.

Hopkins would have argued that happiness lies in aligning our desires to the divine purposes, living within the law, but others find it in precisely the opposite, in throwing off constraint for the intoxication of freedom. The poet Olive Runner (how aptly named) stands at the starting line of the long straight road that invites her to set off at a sprint without knowing where the finishing line will be. In forward motion, under her own power, on an unplanned route, she becomes the brook that flows into the river that flows into the sea, losing herself in hurtling nature. Of course, we do not really do that, or not until we die, but the anticipation at the start of such an adventure is one of the most intense experiences of happiness there is. The high-flying airman in John Gillespie Magee Jr's famous poem feels this too, flinging his Spitfire Mk 1 through 'footless halls of air', liberated from 'the surly bonds of Earth', in a transport, literally, of delight. Short-lived delight, for Magee was killed in a mid-air collision aged only nineteen, the same age as Digby Dolben; another immeasurable loss to poetry in English. His surrender to Earth's surly bonds, and the realization that brooks and tributaries and estuaries and oceans have their own purposes to which ours must adapt, is the bad weather waiting for us somewhere beyond the far horizon.

But the inexorable dynamics of nature may be fought, and there is another kind of happiness that comes from adversity, from defeating it, or discovering in defeat that the battle was not what you thought it was and an unexpected victory yours. W. E. Henley's 'Invictus', anthologized from the moment of publication, has found a new audience recently since Prince Harry, in his work with disabled veterans, chose it for the Invictus Games. Henley wrote it after losing a leg to tuberculosis and undergoing an agonizing series of operations to save the other (the poem's title was actually an invention of Sir Arthur Quiller-Couch, who anthologized it in *The Oxford Book of English Verse*). Ever since, its stoicism, and the promise that even terrible misfortune may be overcome by determination and purpose, has inspired readers, even in these times which seem very distant from the High Victorian world in which it was written. It has been quoted approvingly by two Nobel Peace Prize laureates, Nelson Mandela and Aung San Suu Kyi, and, I'm afraid, the Oklahoma bomber Timothy McVeigh, which tells you how powerful is the human drive to ennoble what we consider to be our struggles.

Nature and society offer their own distinctive opportunities for happiness too. For many, happiness in its paradisal form is associated with nature, finding ourselves at one with it, with ourselves, with God even. Who has not, in moments of crisis or challenge, fantasized about a refuge, a picturesque prelapsarian spot, where we may alone cultivate our garden to the murmuring of innumerable bees? I'm not sure about building a shed 'of clay and wattles', but everything else about Yeats's 'Lake Isle of Innisfree' sounds good to me, and whenever I can I take off to my own version of Yeats's cabin, a tiny corrugated iron hut on a distant beach, where oyster catchers rather than linnets provide the song and midges rather than bees provide aerial distractions. But I know that I am no less a creature of society too, and of course in his great poem Yeats is imagining his island retreat from the heart of the city, with its grey pavements and traffic. Urban happiness is

Introduction

less frequently encountered in poetry, partly because so much English literature (and Irish) took shape in a world where Eden is where we truly belong had we not been banished for our sins. In contrast, the city is frequently a place of temptation or worse. Think of its horrid din in Keats's 'Endymion', a place to leave behind and seek instead the bees humming about 'globes of clover and sweet peas' (bees again), or the London of T. S. Eliot's 'The Waste Land', a sterile and menacing place, where wretched drones trudge over London Bridge to soul-destroying labour in the City. Eliot surely had in mind Wordsworth's poem 'Composed upon Westminster Bridge', written 120 years earlier; but Wordsworth's London is a much more congenial place, a place of promise and freshness and magnificence, and in its way as thrilling a prospect as lofty cliffs and mountain springs. It reminds us too that the old trope that bliss is sylvan is not universally held. St Augustine wrote of the city of God, a place of crowds and industry and neighbours, recalling Jesus in the fourth Gospel speaking of his Father's many-mansioned house. I remember committing what felt like a faux pas once at a Christian Study Day when we were asked to write on a piece of paper what we thought heaven would be like. We handed them in and they were read out by one of the leaders. All were misty mountainsides, and lush meadows, and laughing waterfalls, until mine which read 'the corner of Old Compton Street and Wardour Street'. There were disapproving looks.

Perhaps it is not only happiness that is elusive, but also our efforts to make it mean one big thing rather than a lot of little things. When the Roman Catholic Church produced an English translation of the Latin Bible in the 1960s, it translated the Beatitudes – 'Blessed are they which are persecuted' etc. – as 'happy' rather than 'blessed'. I could see what they meant, the bliss that belongs to the redeemed and is undiminished by cruelty and violence, but to many readers it conjured the unhelpful image of Christians skipping to the arena. The American Constitution, too, recommends the pursuit of happiness as the right of all people as if it were like voting or freedom.

I think happiness is incidental, something we experience when life treats us well, when we are surprised by something wonderful and unexpected, when we have moments of feeling fully alive. It is delightful because it is passing, not the steady-state bliss that has Dante's pilgrim floating around geometry – that is something different – but something that comes and goes; it sparks, it fades, it returns, it vanishes, captured for a moment by the genius of Hopkins and Keats and Wordsworth and Henley and Runner, lively on the page and in your mind. May it come your way, and come frequently.

POEMS FOR HAPPINESS

HAPPY THOUGHT

Happy Thought

The world is so full
 of a number of things,
I'm sure we should all
 be as happy as kings.

Robert Louis Stevenson (1850–1894)

Happy the Man

Happy the man, and happy he alone,
  He who can call today his own;
He who, secure within, can say,
  Tomorrow, do thy worst, for I have lived today.

John Dryden (1631–1700)

New Sights

I like to see a thing I know
Has not been seen before,
That's why I cut my apple through
To look into the core.

It's nice to think, though many an eye
Has seen the ruddy skin,
Mine is the very first to spy
The five brown pips within.

Anon.

On a Quiet Conscience

Close thine eyes, and sleep secure:
Thy soul is safe, thy body pure.
He that guards thee, He that keeps,
Never slumbers, never sleeps.
A quiet conscience, in a quiet breast
Has only peace, has only rest:
The wisest and the mirth of kings
Are out of tune unless she sings.
Then close thine eyes in peace, and sleep secure,
No sleep so sweet as thine, no rest so sure.

Charles I (1600–1649)

Leisure

What is this life if, full of care,
We have no time to stand and stare?

No time to stand beneath the boughs
And stare as long as sheep or cows.

No time to see, when woods we pass,
Where squirrels hide their nuts in grass.

No time to see, in broad daylight,
Streams full of stars, like skies at night.

No time to turn at Beauty's glance,
And watch her feet, how they can dance.

No time to wait till her mouth can
Enrich that smile her eyes began.

A poor life this is if, full of care,
We have no time to stand and stare.

W. H. Davies (1871–1940)

High Flight

Oh! I have slipped the surly bonds of Earth
And danced the skies on laughter-silvered wings;
Sunward I've climbed, and joined the tumbling mirth
Of sun-split clouds, and done a hundred things
You have not dreamed of: wheeled and soared and swung
High in the sunlit silence. Hov'ring there,
I've chased the shouting wind along, and flung
My eager craft through footless halls of air ...
Up, up the long, delirious, burning blue
I've topped the wind-swept heights with easy grace
Where never lark nor even eagle flew
And, while with silent lifting mind I've trod
The high untrespassed sanctity of space,
Put out my hand, and touched the face of God.

John Gillespie Magee Jr (1922–1941)

May the Road Rise Up to Meet You

May the road rise up to meet you.
May the wind be always at your back.
May the sun shine warm upon your face;
The rains fall soft upon your fields.
And until we meet again,
May God hold you in the palm of His hand.

Anon.

If

If you can keep your head when all about you
    Are losing theirs and blaming it on you;
If you can trust yourself when all men doubt you,
    But make allowance for their doubting too;
If you can wait and not be tired by waiting,
    Or being lied about, don't deal in lies,
Or being hated, don't give way to hating,
    And yet don't look too good, nor talk too wise:

If you can dream – and not make dreams your master;
    If you can think – and not make thoughts your aim;
If you can meet with Triumph and Disaster
    And treat those two impostors just the same;
If you can bear to hear the truth you've spoken
    Twisted by knaves to make a trap for fools,
Or watch the things you gave your life to, broken,
    And stoop and build 'em up with worn-out tools:

If you can make one heap of all your winnings
    And risk it on one turn of pitch-and-toss,
And lose, and start again at your beginnings
    And never breathe a word about your loss;
If you can force your heart and nerve and sinew
    To serve your turn long after they are gone,
And so hold on when there is nothing in you
    Except the Will which says to them: 'Hold on!'

If you can talk with crowds and keep your virtue,
   Or walk with Kings – nor lose the common
      touch,
If neither foes nor loving friends can hurt you,
   If all men count with you, but none too much;
If you can fill the unforgiving minute
   With sixty seconds' worth of distance run,
Yours is the Earth and everything that's in it,
   And – which is more – you'll be a Man, my son!

Rudyard Kipling (1865–1936)

Now May Every Living Thing

Now may every living thing, young or old,
weak or strong, living near or far, known or
unknown, living or departed or yet unborn,
may every living thing be full of bliss.

Anon.

Hurt No Living Thing

Hurt no living thing,
Ladybird nor butterfly,
Nor moth with dusty wing,
Nor cricket chirping cheerily,
Nor grasshopper, so light of leap,
Nor dancing gnat,
Nor beetle fat,
Nor harmless worms that creep.

Christina Rossetti (1830–1894)

from Auguries of Innocence

To see a World in a Grain of Sand
And a Heaven in a Wild Flower
Hold Infinity in the palm of your hand
And Eternity in an hour

William Blake (1757–1827)

To Every Thing There Is a Season

To every thing there is a season,
and a time to every purpose under the heaven:
A time to be born, and a time to die;
A time to plant, and a time to pluck up that which is planted;
A time to kill, and a time to heal;
A time to break down, and a time to build up;
A time to weep, and a time to laugh;
A time to mourn, and a time to dance;
A time to cast away stones, and a time to gather stones together;
A time to embrace, and a time to refrain from embracing;
A time to get, and a time to lose;
A time to keep, and a time to cast away;
A time to rend, and a time to sew;
A time to keep silence, and a time to speak;
A time to love, and a time to hate;
A time of war, and a time of peace.

Book of Ecclesiastes

from Endymion

A thing of beauty is a joy for ever:
Its loveliness increases; it will never
Pass into nothingness; but still will keep
A bower quiet for us, and a sleep
Full of sweet dreams, and health, and quiet breathing.
Therefore, on every morrow, are we wreathing
A flowery band to bind us to the earth,
Spite of despondence, of the inhuman dearth
Of noble natures, of the gloomy days,
Of all the unhealthy and o'er-darkened ways
Made for our searching: yes, in spite of all,
Some shape of beauty moves away the pall
From our dark spirits. Such the sun, the moon,
Trees old, and young, sprouting a shady boon
For simple sheep; and such are daffodils
With the green world they live in; and clear rills
That for themselves a cooling covert make
'Gainst the hot season; the mid forest brake,
Rich with a sprinkling of fair musk-rose blooms:
And such too is the grandeur of the dooms
We have imagined for the mighty dead;
All lovely tales that we have heard or read:
An endless fountain of immortal drink,
Pouring unto us from the heaven's brink.

John Keats (1795–1821)

Shining Things

I love all shining things –
      the lovely moon,
The silver stars at night,
      gold sun at noon.
A glowing rainbow in
      a stormy sky,
Or bright clouds hurrying
      when wind goes by.

I love the glow-worm's elf-light
      in the lane,
And leaves a-shine with glistening
      drops of rain,
The glinting wings of bees,
      and butterflies,
My purring pussy's green
      and shining eyes.

I love the street-lamps shining
      through the gloom,
Tall candles lighted in
      a shadowy room,
New-tumbled chestnuts from
      the chestnut tree,
And gleaming fairy bubbles
      blown by me.

I love the shining buttons
      on my coat,
I love the bright beads round
      my mother's throat.

I love the coppery flames
    of red and gold,
That cheer and comfort me,
    when I'm a-cold.

The beauty of all shining things
    is yours and mine,
It was a lovely thought of God
    to make things shine.

Elizabeth Gould (1804–1841)

The Quiet Life

Happy the man, whose wish and care
A few paternal acres bound,
Content to breathe his native air
    In his own ground.

Whose herds with milk, whose fields with bread,
Whose flocks supply him with attire;
Whose trees in summer yield him shade,
    In winter, fire.

Blest, who can unconcern'dly find
Hours, days, and years, slide soft away
In health of body, peace of mind,
    Quiet by day.

Sound sleep by night; study and ease
Together mix'd; sweet recreation,
And innocence, which most does please
    With meditation.

Thus let me live, unseen, unknown;
Thus unlamented let me die;
Steal from the world, and not a stone
    Tell where I lie.

Alexander Pope (1688–1744)

Song of Apollo

The sleepless Hours who watch me as I lie
   Curtained with star-enwoven tapestries
From the broad moonlight of the open sky,
   Fanning the busy dreams from my dim eyes, –
Waken me when their mother, the grey Dawn,
Tells them that dreams and that the moon is gone.

Then I arise; and climbing Heaven's blue dome,
   I walk over the mountains and the waves,
Leaving my robe upon the ocean foam;
   My footsteps pave the clouds with fire; the caves
Are filled with my bright presence, and the air
Leaves the green Earth to my embraces bare.

The sunbeams are my shafts with which I kill
   Deceit, that loves the night and fears the day;
All men who do, or even imagine ill
   Fly me; and from the glory of my ray
Good minds and open actions take new might,
Until diminished by the reign of night.

I feed the clouds, the rainbows and the flowers
   With their aethereal colours; the moon's globe
And the pure stars in their eternal bowers
   Are cinctured with my power as with a robe;
Whatever lamps on Earth or Heaven may shine
Are portions of one spirit; which is mine.

I stand at noon upon the peak of Heaven;
  Then with unwilling steps, I linger down
Into the clouds of the Atlantic even;
  For grief that I depart they weep and frown –
What look is more delightful, than the smile
With which I soothe them from the Western isle?

I am the eye with which the Universe
  Beholds itself, and knows it is divine;
All harmony of instrument and verse,
  All prophecy and medicine are mine,
All light of art or nature: – to my song
Victory and praise, in its own right, belong.

Percy Bysshe Shelley (1792–1822)

My Mind to Me a Kingdom Is

My mind to me a kingdom is;
   Such perfect joy therein I find
That it excels all other bliss
   That world affords or grows by kind.
Though much I want which most would have,
Yet still my mind forbids to crave.

No princely pomp, no wealthy store,
   No force to win the victory,
No wily wit to salve a sore,
   No shape to feed a loving eye;
To none of these I yield as thrall.
For why? my mind doth serve for all.

I see how plenty suffers oft,
   And hasty climbers soon do fall;
I see that those which are aloft
   Mishap doth threaten most of all;
They get with toil, they keep with fear;
Such cares my mind could never bear.

Content I live, this is my stay.
   I seek no more than may suffice;
I press to bear no haughty sway;
   Look, what I lack my mind supplies.
Lo, thus I triumph like a king,
Content with that my mind doth bring.

Some have too much, yet still do crave;
   I little have, and seek no more.
They are but poor, though much they have,
   And I am rich with little store.
They poor, I rich; they beg, I give;
They lack, I leave; they pine, I live.

I laugh not at another's loss;
   I grudge not at another's gain;
No worldly waves my mind can toss;
   My state at one doth still remain.
I fear no foe, I fawn no friend;
I loathe not life, nor dread no end.

Some weigh their pleasure by their lust,
   Their wisdom by their rage of will;
Their treasure is their only trust,
   A cloaked craft their store of skill.
But all the pleasure that I find
Is to maintain a quiet mind.

My wealth is health and perfect ease;
   My conscience clear my chief defence;
I neither seek by bribes to please,
   Nor by desert to breed offence.
Thus do I live, thus will I die;
Would all did so, as well as I.

Sir Edward Dyer (c. 1545–1607)

On First Looking into Chapman's Homer

Much have I travell'd in the realms of gold,
   And many goodly states and kingdoms seen;
   Round many western islands have I been
Which bards in fealty to Apollo hold.
Oft of one wide expanse had I been told
   That deep-brow'd Homer ruled as his demesne;
   Yet did I never breathe its pure serene
Till I heard Chapman speak out loud and bold:
Then felt I like some watcher of the skies
   When a new planet swims into his ken;
Or like stout Cortez when with eagle eyes
   He star'd at the Pacific – and all his men
Look'd at each other with a wild surmise –
   Silent, upon a peak in Darien.

John Keats (1795–1821)

Eternity

He who binds to himself a joy
Does the winged life destroy
He who kisses the joy as it flies
Lives in eternity's sunrise

William Blake (1757–1827)

A Farewell

My fairest child, I have no song to give you;
   No lark could pipe to skies so dull and gray;
Yet, ere we part, one lesson I can leave you
      For every day.

Be good, sweet maid, and let who will be clever;
   Do noble things, not dream them, all day long:
And so make life, death, and that vast forever
      One grand, sweet song.

Charles Kingsley (1819–1875)

A Vision

I saw Eternity the other night,
Like a great ring of pure and endless light,
  All calm, as it was bright: –
And round beneath it, Time, in hours, days, years,
  Driven by the spheres,
Like a vast shadow moved; in which the World
  And all her train were hurl'd.

Henry Vaughan (1622–1695)

Gratefulnesse

Thou that hast giv'n so much to me,
Give one thing more, a gratefull heart.
See how thy beggar works on thee
                          By art.

He makes thy gifts occasion more,
And sayes, If he in this be crost,
All thou hast giv'n him heretofore
                          Is lost.

But thou didst reckon, when at first
Thy word our hearts and hands did crave,
What it would come to at the worst
                          To save.

Perpetuall knockings at thy doore,
Tears sullying thy transparent rooms,
Gift upon gift, much would have more,
                          And comes.

This notwithstanding, thou wentst on,
And didst allow us all our noise:
Nay, thou hast made a sigh and grone
                          Thy joyes.

Not that thou hast not still above
Much better tunes, then grones can make;
But that these countrey-aires thy love
                          Did take.

Wherefore I crie, and crie again;
And in no quiet canst thou be,
Till I a thankfull heart obtain
                    Of thee:

Not thankfull, when it pleaseth me;
As if thy blessings had spare dayes:
But such a heart, whose pulse may be
                    Thy praise.

George Herbert (1593–1633)

Thanks in Old Age

Thanks in old age – thanks ere I go,
For health, the midday sun, the impalpable
   air – for life, mere life,
For precious ever-lingering memories, (of you
   my mother dear – you, father – you, brothers,
   sisters, friends,)
For all my days – not those of peace alone – the
   days of war the same,
For gentle words, caresses, gifts from foreign lands,
For shelter, wine and meat – for sweet appreciation,
(You distant, dim unknown – or young or
   old – countless, unspecified, readers belov'd,
We never met, and ne'er shall meet – and yet
   our souls embrace, long, close and long;)
For beings, groups, love, deeds, words, books – for
   colors, forms,
For all the brave strong men – devoted, hardy
   men – who've forward sprung in freedom's help,
   all years, all lands,
For braver, stronger, more devoted men – (a
   special laurel ere I go, to life's war's chosen ones,
The cannoneers of song and thought – the
   great artillerists – the foremost leaders,
   captains of the soul:)
As soldier from an ended war return'd – As traveler
   out of myriads, to the long procession retrospective,
Thanks – joyful thanks! – a soldier's, traveler's thanks.

Walt Whitman (1819–1892)

A Little Health

A little health,
A little wealth,
A little house and freedom,
And at the end
A little friend
And little cause to need him.

Anon.

GLORY BE TO GOD FOR
DAPPLED THINGS

Pied Beauty

Glory be to God for dappled things –
   For skies of couple-colour as a brinded cow;
      For rose-moles all in stipple upon trout that swim;
Fresh-firecoal chestnut-falls; finches' wings;
   Landscape plotted and pieced – fold, fallow, and plough;
      And áll trádes, their gear and tackle and trim.

All things counter, original, spare, strange;
   Whatever is fickle, freckled (who knows how?)
      With swift, slow; sweet, sour; adazzle, dim;
He fathers-forth whose beauty is past change:
            Praise him.

Gerard Manley Hopkins (1844–1889)

Amazing Grace

Amazing grace, how sweet the sound
That saved a wretch like me.
I once was lost, but now I am found,
Was blind, but now I see.

'Twas grace that taught my heart to fear,
And grace my fears relieved.
How precious did that grace appear
The hour I first believed.

Through many dangers, toils and snares
I have already come,
'Tis grace has brought me safe thus far
And grace will lead me home.

The Lord has promised good to me,
His word my hope secures;
He will my shield and portion be,
As long as life endures.

Yea, when this flesh and heart shall fail,
And mortal life shall cease,
I shall possess within the veil,
A life of joy and peace.

When we've been there ten thousand years
Bright shining as the sun,
We've no less days to sing God's praise
Than when we've first begun.

John Newton (1725–1807)

God Be In My Head

God be in my head
And in my understanding;
God be in myne eyes,
And in my looking;
God be in my mouth,
And in my speaking;
God be in my heart,
And in my thynking;
God be at my end,
And at my departing.

Sarum Missal
(Eleventh Century)

'Lord, make me an instrument of Thy peace'

Lord, make me an instrument of Thy peace.
Where there is hatred, let me sow love;
Where there is injury, pardon;
Where there is doubt, faith;
When there is despair, hope;
Where there is darkness, light;
When there is sadness, joy.

O Divine Master, grant that
I may not so much seek
To be consoled, as to console;
Not so much to be understood as
To understand; not so much to be
Loved as to love:
For it is in giving that we receive;
It is in pardoning, that we are pardoned;
It is in dying, that we awaken to eternal life.

St Francis of Assisi (1182–1226)

Miracles

Why, who makes much of a miracle?
As to me I know of nothing else but miracles,
Whether I walk the streets of Manhattan,
Or dart my sight over the roofs of houses toward the sky,
Or wade with naked feet along the beach just in
   the edge of the water,
Or stand under trees in the woods,
Or talk by day with any one I love, or sleep in the
   bed at night with any one I love,
Or sit at table at dinner with the rest,
Or look at strangers opposite me riding in the car,
Or watch honey-bees busy around the hive of a
   summer forenoon,
Or animals feeding in the fields,
Or birds, or the wonderfulness of insects in the air,
Or the wonderfulness of the sundown, or of stars
   shining so quiet and bright,
Or the exquisite delicate thin curve of the new
   moon in spring;
These with the rest, one and all, are to me miracles,
The whole referring, yet each distinct and in its place.
To me every hour of the light and dark is a miracle,
Every cubic inch of space is a miracle,
Every square yard of the surface of the earth is
   spread with the same,
Every foot of the interior swarms with the same.
To me the sea is a continual miracle,
The fishes that swim – the rocks – the motion of
   the waves – the ships with men in them,
What stranger miracles are there?

Walt Whitman (1819–1892)

Father, We Thank Thee

For flowers that bloom about our feet,
   Father, we thank Thee,
For tender grass so fresh and sweet,
   Father, we thank Thee,
For the song of bird and hum of bee,
For all things fair we hear or see,
Father in heaven, we thank Thee.

For blue of stream and blue of sky,
   Father, we thank Thee,
For pleasant shade of branches high,
   Father, we thank Thee,
For fragrant air and cooling breeze,
For beauty of the blooming trees,
Father in heaven, we thank Thee.

For this new morning with its light,
   Father, we thank Thee,
For rest and shelter of the night,
   Father, we thank Thee,
For health and food, for love and friends,
For everything Thy goodness sends,
Father in heaven, we thank Thee.

Ralph Waldo Emerson (1803–1882)

African Canticle

All you *big* things, bless the Lord
Mount Kilimanjaro and Lake Victoria
The Rift Valley and the Serengeti Plain
Fat baobabs and shady mango trees
All eucalyptus and tamarind trees
Bless the Lord
Praise and extol Him for ever and ever.

All you *tiny* things, bless the Lord
Busy black ants and hopping fleas
Wriggling tadpoles and mosquito larvae
Flying locusts and water drops
Pollen dust and tsetse flies
Millet seeds and dried dagaa
Bless the Lord
Praise and extol Him for ever and ever.

Anon.

The Thanksgivings

We who are here present thank the Great Spirit that
we are here to praise Him.
We thank Him that He has created men and women,
and ordered that these beings shall always be living
to multiply the earth.
We thank Him for making the earth and giving
these beings its products to live on.
We thank Him for the water that comes out of
the earth and runs for our lands.
We thank Him for all the animals on the earth.
We thank Him for certain timbers that grow and
have fluids coming from them for us all.
We thank Him for the branches of the trees that
grow shadows for our shelter.
We thank Him for the beings that come from the
west, the thunder and lightning that water the earth.
We thank Him for the light which we call our oldest
brother, the sun that works for our good.
We thank Him for all the fruits that grow on the
trees and vines.
We thank Him for his goodness in making the forests,
and thank all its trees.
We thank Him for the darkness that gives us rest, and
for the kind Being of the darkness that gives us
light, the moon.
We thank Him for the bright spots in the skies that
give us signs, the stars.
We give Him thanks for our supporters, who had
charge of our harvests.
We give thanks that the voice of the Great Spirit can
still be heard through the words of Ga-ne-o-di-o.

We thank the Great Spirit that we have the privilege
  of this pleasant occasion.
We give thanks for the persons who can sing the
  Great Spirit's music, and hope they will be
  privileged to continue in his faith.
We thank the Great Spirit for all the persons who
  perform the ceremonies on this occasion.

Iroquois, Traditional
tr. Harriet Maxwell Converse (1836–1903)

Harvest Home

Come, ye thankful people, come,
Raise the song of harvest home:
All is safely gathered in,
Ere the winter storms begin;
God, our Maker, doth provide
For our wants to be supplied:
Come to God's own temple, come,
Raise the song of harvest home.

All the world is God's own field,
Fruit unto His praise to yield;
Wheat and tares together sown,
Unto joy or sorrow grown;
First the blade, and then the ear,
Then the full corn shall appear:
Lord of harvest, grant that we
Wholesome grain and pure may be.

For the Lord our God shall come,
And shall take His harvest home;
From His field shall in that day
All offenses purge away;
Give His angels charge at last
In the fire the tares to cast;
But the fruitful ears to store
In His garner evermore.

Even so, Lord, quickly come
To Thy final harvest home;
Gather Thou Thy people in,
Free from sorrow, free from sin;

There, forever purified,
In Thy presence to abide:
Come, with all Thine angels, come,
Raise the glorious harvest home.

Henry Alford (1810–1871)

Swing Low, Sweet Chariot

Swing low, sweet chariot
Coming for to carry me home,
Swing low, sweet chariot,
Coming for to carry me home.

I looked over Jordan, and what did I see
Coming for to carry me home?
A band of angels coming after me,
Coming for to carry me home.

Sometimes I'm up, and sometimes I'm down,
(Coming for to carry me home)
But still my soul feels heavenly bound.
(Coming for to carry me home)

The brightest day that I can say,
(Coming for to carry me home)
When Jesus washed my sins away.
(Coming for to carry me home)

If you get there before I do,
(Coming for to carry me home)
Tell all my friends I'm coming there too.
(Coming for to carry me home)

Wallace Willis

Desiderata

Go placidly amid the noise and haste,
and remember what peace there may be in silence.
As far as possible without surrender
be on good terms with all persons.
Speak your truth quietly and clearly;
and listen to others,
even the dull and the ignorant;
they too have their story.

Avoid loud and aggressive persons,
they are vexations to the spirit.
If you compare yourself with others,
you may become vain and bitter;
for always there will be greater and lesser persons
 than yourself.
Enjoy your achievements as well as your plans.

Keep interested in your own career, however humble;
it is a real possession in the changing fortunes of time.
Exercise caution in your business affairs;
for the world is full of trickery.
But let this not blind you to what virtue there is;
many persons strive for high ideals;
and everywhere life is full of heroism.

Be yourself.
Especially, do not feign affection.
Neither be cynical about love;
for in the face of all aridity and disenchantment
it is as perennial as the grass.
Take kindly the counsel of the years,

gracefully surrendering the things of youth.
Nurture strength of spirit to shield you in sudden
   misfortune.
But do not distress yourself with dark imaginings.
Many fears are born of fatigue and loneliness.
Beyond a wholesome discipline,
be gentle with yourself.

You are a child of the universe,
no less than the trees and the stars;
you have a right to be here.
And whether or not it is clear to you,
no doubt the universe is unfolding as it should.

Therefore be at peace with God,
whatever you conceive Him to be,
and whatever your labors and aspirations,
in the noisy confusion of life keep peace with your soul.

With all its sham, drudgery, and broken dreams,
it is still a beautiful world.
Be cheerful.
Strive to be happy.

Max Ehrmann (1872–1945)

The Iroquois Prayer

We return thanks to our mother, the earth, which sustains us.
We return thanks to the rivers and streams, which supply us with water.
We return thanks to all herbs, which furnish medicines for the cure of our diseases.
We return thanks to the corn, and to her sisters, the beans and squash, which give us life.
We return thanks to the bushes and trees, which provide us with fruit.
We return thanks to the wind which, moving the air, has banished diseases.
We return thanks to the moon and the stars, which have given us their light when the sun was gone.
We return thanks to our grandfather He-no, who has given to us his rain.
We return thanks to the sun, that he has looked upon the earth with a beneficent eye.
Lastly, we return thanks to the Great Spirit, in whom is embodied all goodness, and who directs all things for the good of his children.

Iroquois, Traditional

Jewish Prayer

Though our mouths were full of song as the sea,
Our tongues of exultation as the fullness of its waves,
And our lips of praise as the plains of the firmament:

Though our eyes gave light as the sun and moon:
Though our hands were outspread as the eagles
 of heaven,
And our feet were swift as hinds,

Yet should we be unable to thank Thee,
O Lord our God and God of our fathers,
And to bless Thy Name for even one of the countless
 thousands
And tens of thousands
Of kindnesses which Thou hast done by our fathers
 and by us.

Service of the Orthodox Synagogue
for the Festival of Tabernacles

from His Pilgrimage

Give me my scallop-shell of quiet,
My staff of faith to walk upon,
My scrip of joy, immortal diet,
My bottle of salvation,
My gown of Glory, hope's true gage;
And thus I'll take my pilgrimage.

Sir Walter Raleigh (c. 1554–1618)

When the Heart is Hard

When the heart is hard and parched up, come upon
  me with a shower of mercy.
When grace is lost from life, come with a burst of
  song.
When tumultuous work raises its din on all sides
  shutting me out from beyond, come to me, my
  lord of silence, with thy peace and rest.
When my beggarly heart sits crouched, shut up in a
  corner, break open the door, my king, and come
  with the ceremony of a king.
When desire blinds the mind with delusion and dust,
  O thou holy one, thou wakeful, come with thy light
  and thy thunder.

Rabindranath Tagore (1861–1941)

The Selkirk Grace

Some have meat and cannot eat,
  Some cannot eat that want it:
But we have meat and we can eat,
  Sae let the Lord be thankit.

Robert Burns (1759–1796)

Epitaph

God give me work
Till my life shall end
And life
Till my work is done.

Winifred Holtby (1898–1935)

I SING OF BROOKS, OF
BLOSSOMS, BIRDS, AND BOWERS

The Argument of His Book

I sing of brooks, of blossoms, birds, and bowers,
Of April, May, of June, and July flowers.
I sing of May-poles, hock-carts, wassails, wakes,
Of bridegrooms, brides, and of their bridal-cakes.
I write of youth, of love, and have access
By these to sing of cleanly wantonness.
I sing of dews, of rains, and piece by piece
Of balm, of oil, of spice, and ambergris.
I sing of Time's trans-shifting; and I write
How roses first came red, and lilies white.
I write of groves, of twilights, and I sing
The court of Mab, and of the fairy king.
I write of Hell; I sing (and ever shall)
Of Heaven, and hope to have it after all.

Robert Herrick (1591–1674)

The Song of Wandering Aengus

I went out to the hazel wood,
Because a fire was in my head,
And cut and peeled a hazel wand,
And hooked a berry to a thread;
And when white moths were on the wing,
And moth-like stars were flickering out,
I dropped the berry in a stream
And caught a little silver trout.

When I had laid it on the floor
I went to blow the fire aflame,
But something rustled on the floor,
And someone called me by my name;
It had become a glimmering girl
With apple blossom in her hair
Who called me by my name and ran
And faded through the brightening air.

Though I am old with wandering
Through hollow lands and hilly lands,
I will find out where she has gone,
And kiss her lips and take her hands;
And walk among long dappled grass,
And pluck till time and times are done,
The silver apples of the moon,
The golden apples of the sun.

W. B. Yeats (1865–1939)

Spring

Sound the Flute!
Now it's mute.
Birds delight
Day and Night;
Nightingale
In the dale
Lark in Sky,
Merrily,
Merrily, Merrily, to welcome in the Year.

Little Boy,
Full of joy;
Little Girl,
Sweet and small;
Cock does crow,
So do you;
Merry voice,
Infant noise,
Merrily, Merrily, to welcome in the Year.

Little Lamb,
Here I am;
Come and lick
My white neck;
Let me pull
Your soft Wool;
Let me kiss
Your soft face:
Merrily, Merrily, we welcome in the Year.

William Blake (1757–1827)

I Wandered Lonely as a Cloud

I wandered lonely as a cloud
That floats on high o'er vales and hills,
When all at once I saw a crowd,
A host, of golden daffodils;
Beside the lake, beneath the trees,
Fluttering and dancing in the breeze.

Continuous as the stars that shine
And twinkle on the milky way,
They stretched in never-ending line
Along the margin of a bay:
Ten thousand saw I at a glance,
Tossing their heads in sprightly dance.

The waves beside them danced; but they
Out-did the sparkling waves in glee:
A poet could not but be gay,
In such a jocund company:
I gazed – and gazed – but little thought
What wealth the show to me had brought:

For oft, when on my couch I lie
In vacant or in pensive mood,
They flash upon that inward eye
Which is the bliss of solitude;
And then my heart with pleasure fills,
And dances with the daffodils.

William Wordsworth (1770–1850)

I'll Tell You How the Sun Rose

I'll tell you how the Sun rose –
A Ribbon at a time –
The Steeples swam in Amethyst –
The news, like Squirrels, ran –
The Hills untied their Bonnets –
The Bobolinks – begun –
Then I said softly to myself –
'That must have been the Sun'!
But how he set – I know not –
There seemed a purple stile
That little Yellow boys and girls
Were climbing all the while –
Till when they reached the other side,
A Dominie in Gray –
Put gently up the evening Bars –
And led the flock away –

Emily Dickinson (1830–1886)

The Happy Child

I saw this day sweet flowers grow thick –
But not one like the child did pick.

I heard the pack-hounds in green park –
But no dog like the child heard bark.

I heard this day bird after bird –
But not one like the child has heard.

A hundred butterflies saw I –
But not one like the child saw fly.

I saw horses roll in grass –
But no horse like the child saw pass.

My world this day has lovely been –
But not like what the child has seen.

W. H. Davies (1871–1940)

from Pippa Passes

The year's at the spring
And day's at the morn;
Morning's at seven;
The hillside's dew-pearled;
The lark's on the wing;
The snail's on the thorn:
God's in His heaven—
All's right with the world!

Robert Browning (1812–1889)

A Greeting

Good morning, Life – and all
Things glad and beautiful.
My pockets nothing hold,
But he that owns the gold,
The Sun, is my great friend –
His spending has no end.

Hail to the morning sky,
Whose bright clouds measure high;
Hail to you birds whose throats
Would number leaves by notes;
Hail to you shady bowers,
And you green fields of flowers.

Hail to you women fair,
That make a show so rare
In cloth as white as milk –
Be't calico or silk:
Good morning, Life – and all
Things glad and beautiful.

W. H. Davies (1871–1940)

February Twilight

I stood beside a hill
  Smooth with new-laid snow,
A single star looked out
  From the cold evening glow.

There was no other creature
  That saw what I could see –
I stood and watched the evening star
  As long as it watched me.

Sara Teasdale (1884–1933)

Adoration

For ADORATION seasons change,
And order, truth, and beauty range,
  Adjust, attract, and fill:
The grass the polyanthus cheques;
And polish'd porphyry reflects,
  By the descending rill.

Rich almonds colour to the prime
For ADORATION; tendrils climb,
  And fruit-trees pledge their gems;
And Ivis, with her gorgeous vest,
Builds for her eggs her cunning nest,
  And bell-flowers bow their stems.

Now labour his reward receives,
For ADORATION counts his sheaves,
  To peace, her bounteous prince;
The nectarine his strong tint imbibes,
And apples of ten thousand tribes,
  And quick peculiar quince.

Christopher Smart (1722–1771)

The Sun Rising

    Busy old fool, unruly sun,
       Why dost thou thus,
Through windows, and through curtains call on us?
Must to thy motions lovers' seasons run?
      Saucy pedantic wretch, go chide
      Late school-boys, and sour prentices,
   Go tell court-huntsmen, that the King will ride,
   Call country ants to harvest offices;
Love, all alike, no season knows, nor clime,
Nor hours, days, months, which are the rags of time.

     Thy beams, so reverend, and strong
       Why shouldst thou think?
I could eclipse and cloud them with a wink,
But that I would not lose her sight so long:
      If her eyes have not blinded thine,
      Look, and tomorrow late, tell me,
   Whether both th'Indias of spice and mine
   Be where thou left'st them, or lie here with me.
Ask for those kings whom thou saw'st yesterday,
And thou shalt hear, All here in one bed lay.

     She's all states, and all princes, I,
       Nothing else is.
Princes do but play us; compared to this,
All honour's mimic; all wealth alchemy.
      Thou sun art half as happy as we,
      In that the world's contracted thus;

Thine age asks ease, and since thy duties be
To warm the world, that's done in warming us.
Shine here to us, and thou art everywhere;
This bed thy centre is, these walls, thy sphere.

John Donne (c. 1572–1631)

Sowing

It was a perfect day
For sowing; just
As sweet and dry was the ground
As tobacco-dust.

I tasted deep the hour
Between the far
Owl's chuckling first soft cry
And the first star.

A long stretched hour it was;
Nothing undone
Remained; the early seeds
All safely sown.

And now, hark at the rain,
Windless and light,
Half a kiss, half a tear,
Saying good-night.

Edward Thomas (1878–1917)

A Dumb Friend

I planted a young tree when I was young:
But now the tree is grown and I am old:
There wintry robin shelters from the cold
    And tunes his silver tongue.

A green and living tree I planted it,
A glossy-foliaged tree of evergreen:
All through the noontide heat it spread a screen
    Whereunder I might sit.

But now I only watch it where it towers:
I, sitting at my window, watch it tost
By rattling gale or silvered by the frost;
    Or, when sweet summer flowers,

Wagging its round green head with stately grace
In tender winds that kiss it and go by.
It shows a green full age: and what show I?
    A faded wrinkled face.

So often have I watched it, till mine eyes
Have filled with tears and I have ceased to see,
That now it seems a very friend to me,
    In all my secrets wise.

A faithful pleasant friend, who year by year
Grew with my growth and strengthened with my strength,
But whose green lifetime shows a longer length;
    When I shall not sit here

It still will bud in spring, and shed rare leaves
In autumn, and in summer-heat give shade,
And warmth in winter: when my bed is made
    In shade the cypress weaves.

Christina Rossetti (1830–1894)

My Heart Leaps Up

My heart leaps up when I behold
  A rainbow in the sky:
So was it when my life began;
So is it now I am a man;
So be it when I shall grow old,
  Or let me die!
The Child is father of the Man;
And I could wish my days to be
Bound each to each by natural piety.

William Wordsworth (1770–1850)

The Throstle

'Summer is coming, summer is coming.
  I know it, I know it, I know it.
Light again, leaf again, life again, love again,'
  Yes, my wild little Poet.

Sing the new year in under the blue.
  Last year you sang it as gladly.
'New, new, new, new'! Is it then so new
  That you should carol so madly?

'Love again, song again, nest again, young again,'
  Never a prophet so crazy!
And hardly a daisy as yet, little friend,
  See, there is hardly a daisy.

'Here again, here, here, here, happy year'!
  O warble unchidden, unbidden!
Summer is coming, is coming, my dear,
  And all the winters are hidden.

Alfred, Lord Tennyson (1809–1892)

May

O! the month of May, the merry month of May,
   So frolic, so gay, and so green, so green, so green!
O! and then did I unto my true Love say,
   Sweet Peg, thou shalt be my Summer's Queen.

Now the nightingale, the pretty nightingale,
   The sweetest singer in all the forest's choir,
Entreats thee, sweet Peggy, to hear thy true Love's tale:
   Lo! yonder she sitteth, her breast against a briar.

But O! I spy the cuckoo, the cuckoo, the cuckoo;
   See where she sitteth; come away, my joy:
Come away, I prithee, I do not like the cuckoo
   Should sing where my Peggy and I kiss and toy.

O! the month of May, the merry month of May,
   So frolic, so gay, and so green, so green, so green!
And then did I unto my true Love say,
   Sweet Peg, thou shalt be my Summer's Queen.

Thomas Dekker (c. 1570–1632)

Moonlight, Summer Moonlight

'Tis moonlight, summer moonlight,
All soft and still and fair;
The silent time of midnight
Shines sweetly everywhere,

But most where trees are sending
Their breezy boughs on high,
Or stooping low are lending
A shelter from the sky.

Emily Brontë (1818–1848)

The Lake Isle of Innisfree

I will arise and go now, and go to Innisfree,
And a small cabin build there, of clay and wattles made:
Nine bean-rows will I have there, a hive for the honey-bee,
And live alone in the bee-loud glade.

And I shall have some peace there, for peace comes dropping slow,
Dropping from the veils of the morning to where the cricket sings;
There midnight's all a glimmer, and noon a purple glow,
And evening full of the linnet's wings.

I will arise and go now, for always night and day
I hear lake water lapping with low sounds by the shore;
While I stand on the roadway, or on the pavements grey,
I hear it in the deep heart's core.

W. B. Yeats (1865–1939)

Where the Bee Sucks

Where the bee sucks, there suck I:
In a cowslip's bell I lie;
There I couch when owls do cry.
On the bat's back I do fly
After summer merrily.
Merrily, merrily shall I live now
Under the blossom that hangs on the bough.

William Shakespeare (1564–1616)

To Make a Prairie

To make a prairie it takes a clover and one bee,
One clover, and a bee,
And revery.
The revery alone will do,
If bees are few.

Emily Dickinson (1830–1886)

from A Midsummer Night's Dream

I know a bank where the wild thyme blows,
Where oxlips and the nodding violet grows,
Quite over-canopied with luscious woodbine,
With sweet musk-roses and with eglantine:
There sleeps Titania sometime of the night,
Lull'd in these flowers with dances and delight;
And there the snake throws her enamell'd skin,
Weed wide enough to wrap a fairy in:
And with the juice of this I'll streak her eyes,
And make her full of hateful fantasies.
Take thou some of it, and seek through this grove:
A sweet Athenian lady is in love
With a disdainful youth: anoint his eyes;
But do it when the next thing he espies
May be the lady: thou shalt know the man
By the Athenian garments he hath on.
Effect it with some care, that he may prove
More fond on her than she upon her love:
And look thou meet me ere the first cock crow.

William Shakespeare (1564–1616)

Careless Rambles

I love to wander at my idle will
In summer's luscious prime about the fields
And kneel when thirsty at the little rill
To sip the draught its pebbly bottom yields
And where the maple bush its fountain shields
To lie and rest a swailey hour away
And crop the swelling peascod from the land
Or mid the uplands woodland walks to stray
Where oaks for aye o'er their old shadows stand
Neath whose dark foliage with a welcome hand
I pluck the luscious strawberry ripe and red
As beauty's lips – and in my fancy's dreams
As mid the velvet moss I musing tread
Feel life as lovely as her picture seems.

John Clare (1793–1864)

Magna Est Veritas

Here, in this little Bay,
Full of tumultuous life and great repose,
Where, twice a day,
The purposeless, glad ocean comes and goes,
Under high cliffs, and far from the huge town,
I sit me down.
For want of me the world's course will not fail:
When all its work is done, the lie shall rot:
The truth is great, and shall prevail,
When none cares whether it prevail or not.

Coventry Patmore (1823–1896)

Rest and Be Thankful!
(At the head of Glencroe)

Doubling and doubling with laborious walk,
Who, that has gained at length the wished-for Height,
This brief, this simple wayside Call can slight,
And rests not thankful? Whether cheered by talk
With some loved friend, or by the unseen hawk
Whistling to clouds and sky-born streams, that shine
At the sun's outbreak, as with light divine,
Ere they descend to nourish root and stalk
Of valley flowers. Nor, while the limbs repose,
Will we forget that, as the fowl can keep
Absolute stillness, poised aloft in air,
And fishes front, unmoved, the torrent's sweep, –
So may the Soul, through powers that Faith bestows,
Win rest, and ease, and peace, with bliss that Angels share.

William Wordsworth (1770–1850)

Composed Upon Westminster Bridge, September 3, 1802

Earth has not anything to show more fair:
Dull would he be of soul who could pass by
A sight so touching in its majesty:
This City now doth, like a garment, wear
The beauty of the morning; silent, bare,
Ships, towers, domes, theatres, and temples lie
Open unto the fields, and to the sky;
All bright and glittering in the smokeless air.
Never did sun more beautifully steep
In his first splendour, valley, rock, or hill;
Ne'er saw I, never felt, a calm so deep!
The river glideth at his own sweet will:
Dear God! the very houses seem asleep;
And all that mighty heart is lying still!

William Wordsworth (1770–1850)

Moonlit Apples

At the top of the house the apples are laid in rows,
And the skylight lets the moonlight in, and those
Apples are deep-sea apples of green. There goes
    A cloud on the moon in the autumn night.

A mouse in the wainscot scratches, and scratches,
    and then
There is no sound at the top of the house of men
Or mice; and the cloud is blown, and the moon again
    Dapples the apples with deep-sea light.

They are lying in rows there, under the gloomy
    beams;
On the sagging floor; they gather the silver streams
Out of the moon, those moonlit apples of dreams,
    And quiet is the steep stair under.

In the corridors under there is nothing but sleep.
And stiller than ever on orchard boughs they keep
Tryst with the moon, and deep is the silence, deep
    On the moon-washed apples of wonder.

John Drinkwater (1882–1937)

Harvest Hymn

Once more the liberal year laughs out
   O'er richer stores than gems or gold;
Once more with harvest-song and shout
   Is Nature's bloodless triumph told.

Oh, favors every year made new!
   Oh, gifts with rain and sunshine sent!
The bounty overruns our due,
   The fulness shames our discontent.

We shut our eyes, the flowers bloom on;
   We murmur, but the corn-ears fill,
We choose the shadow, but the sun
   That casts it shines behind us still.

Who murmurs at his lot to-day?
   Who scorns his native fruit and bloom?
Or sighs for dainties far away,
   Beside the bounteous board of home?

Thank Heaven, instead, that Freedom's arm
   Can change a rocky soil to gold, –
That brave and generous lives can warm
   A clime with northern ices cold.

And let these altars, wreathed with flowers
   And piled with fruits, awake again
Thanksgivings for the golden hours,
   The early and the latter rain!

John Greenleaf Whittier (1807–1892)

To Autumn

Season of mists and mellow fruitfulness!
  Close bosom-friend of the maturing sun;
Conspiring with him how to load and bless
  With fruit the vines that round the thatch-eaves run;
To bend with apples the moss'd cottage-trees,
  And fill all fruit with ripeness to the core;
    To swell the gourd, and plump the hazel shells
With a sweet kernel; to set budding more,
And still more, later flowers for the bees,
Until they think warm days will never cease,
    For Summer has o'er-brimm'd their clammy cells.

Who hath not seen thee oft amid thy store?
  Sometimes whoever seeks abroad may find
Thee sitting careless on a granary floor,
  Thy hair soft-lifted by the winnowing wind;
Or on a half-reap'd furrow sound asleep,
  Drowsed with the fumes of poppies, while thy hook
    Spares the next swath and all its twinèd flowers;
And sometimes like a gleaner thou dost keep
  Steady thy laden head across a brook;
  Or by a cider-press, with patient look,
    Thou watchest the last oozings, hours by hours.

Where are the songs of Spring? Ay, where are they?
  Think not of them, thou hast thy music too,
While barrèd clouds bloom the soft-dying day,
  And touch the stubble-plains with rosy hue;
Then in a wailful choir the small gnats mourn
  Among the river sallows, borne aloft
    Or sinking as the light wind lives or dies;

And full-grown lambs loud bleat from hilly bourn;
  Hedge-crickets sing; and now with treble soft
The redbreast whistles from a garden-croft,
  And gathering swallows twitter in the skies.

John Keats (1795–1821)

Pleasant Sounds

The rustling of leaves under the feet in woods and
under hedges;
The crumping of cat-ice and snow down wood-rides,
narrow lanes, and every street causeway;
Rustling through a wood or rather rushing, while the
wind halloos in the oak-toop like thunder;
The rustle of birds' wings startled from their nests or
flying unseen into the bushes;
The whizzing of larger birds overhead in a wood, such
as crows, puddocks, buzzards;
The trample of robins and woodlarks on the brown
leaves, and the patter of squirrels on the green moss;
The fall of an acorn on the ground, the pattering of
nuts on the hazel branches as they fall from ripeness;
The flirt of the groundlark's wing from the stubbles –
how sweet such pictures on dewy mornings, when
the dew flashes from its brown feathers.

John Clare (1793–1864)

'See yonder leafless trees against the sky'

See yonder leafless trees against the sky,
How they diffuse themselves into the air,
And ever subdividing separate,
Limbs into branches, branches into twigs,
As if they loved the element & hasted
To dissipate their being into it.

Ralph Waldo Emerson (1803–1882)

Evening Quatrains

The Day's grown old, the fainting Sun
Has but a little way to run,
And yet his Steeds, with all his skill,
Scarce lug the Chariot down the Hill.

With Labour spent, and Thirst opprest,
Whilst they strain hard to gain the West,
From Fetlocks hot drops melted light,
Which turn to Meteors in the Night.

The Shadows now so long do grow,
That Brambles like tall Cedars show,
Mole-hills seem Mountains, and the Ant
Appears a monstrous Elephant.

A very little little Flock
Shades thrice the ground that it would stock;
Whilst the small Stripling following them,
Appears a mighty *Polypheme*.

These being brought into the Fold,
And by the thrifty Master told,
He thinks his Wages are well paid,
Since none are either lost, or stray'd.

Now lowing Herds are each-where heard,
Chains rattle in the Villeins Yard,
The Cart's on Tayl set down to rest,
Bearing on high the Cuckolds Crest.

The hedg is stript, the Clothes brought in,
Nought's left without should be within.
The Bees are hiv'd, and hum their Charm,
Whilst every House does seem a Swarm.

The Cock now to the Roost is prest:
For he must call up all the rest;
The Sow's fast pegg'd within the Sty,
To still her squeaking Progeny.

Each one has had his Supping Mess,
The Cheese is put into the Press,
The Pans and Bowls clean scalded all,
Rear'd up against the Milk-house Wall.

And now on Benches all are sat
In the cool Air to sit and chat,
Till *Phoebus*, dipping in the West,
Shall lead the World the way to Rest.

Charles Cotton (1630–1687)

Ode

The spacious firmament on high,
With all the blue ethereal sky,
And spangled heav'ns, a shining frame,
Their great original proclaim:
Th' unwearied sun, from day to day,
Does his Creator's power display,
And publishes to every land
The work of an almighty hand.

Soon as the evening shades prevail,
The moon takes up the wondrous tale,
And nightly to the list'ning earth
Repeats the story of her birth:
Whilst all the stars that round her burn,
And all the planets in their turn,
Confirm the tidings as they roll,
And spread the truth from pole to pole.

What though, in solemn silence, all
Move round the dark terrestrial ball?
What though nor real voice nor sound
Amid their radiant orbs be found?
In reason's ear they all rejoice,
And utter forth a glorious voice,
For ever singing, as they shine,
'The hand that made us is divine.'

Joseph Addison (1672–1719)

'It is a beauteous evening, calm and free'

It is a beauteous evening, calm and free,
The holy time is quiet as a Nun
Breathless with adoration; the broad sun
Is sinking down in its tranquillity;
The gentleness of heaven broods o'er the Sea:
Listen! the mighty Being is awake,
And doth with his eternal motion make
A sound like thunder – everlastingly.
Dear Child! dear Girl! that walkest with me here,
If thou appear untouched by solemn thought,
Thy nature is not therefore less divine:
Thou liest in Abraham's bosom all the year;
And worshipp'st at the Temple's inner shrine,
God being with thee when we know it not.

William Wordsworth (1770–1850)

God's Grandeur

The world is charged with the grandeur of God.
  It will flame out, like shining from shook foil;
  It gathers to a greatness, like the ooze of oil
Crushed. Why do men then now not reck his rod?
Generations have trod, have trod, have trod;
  And all is seared with trade; bleared, smeared
    with toil;
  And wears man's smudge and shares man's smell:
    the soil
Is bare now, nor can foot feel, being shod.

And for all this, nature is never spent;
  There lives the dearest freshness deep down things;
And though the last lights off the black West went
  Oh, morning, at the brown brink eastward, springs –
Because the Holy Ghost over the bent
  World broods with warm breast and with ah!
    bright wings.

Gerard Manley Hopkins (1844–1889)

SAY NOT THE STRUGGLE
NOUGHT AVAILETH

Say Not the Struggle Nought Availeth

Say not the struggle nought availeth,
  The labour and the wounds are vain,
The enemy faints not, nor faileth,
  And as things have been they remain.

If hopes were dupes, fears may be liars;
  It may be, in yon smoke concealed,
Your comrades chase e'en now the fliers,
  And, but for you, possess the field.

For while the tired waves, vainly breaking,
  Seem here no painful inch to gain,
Far back through creeks and inlets making
  Comes silent, flooding in, the main,

And not by eastern windows only,
  When daylight comes, comes in the light,
In front the sun climbs slow, how slowly,
  But westward, look, the land is bright.

Arthur Hugh Clough (1819–1861)

Freedom

Give me the long, straight road before me,
  A clear, cold day with a nipping air,
Tall, bare trees to run on beside me,
  A heart that is light and free from care.
Then let me go! – I care not whither
  My feet may lead, for my spirit shall be
Free as the brook that flows to the river,
  Free as the river that flows to the sea.

Olive Runner

New Every Morning

Every day is a fresh beginning,
Listen my soul to the glad refrain.
And, spite of old sorrows
And older sinning,
Troubles forecasted
And possible pain,
Take heart with the day and begin again.

Susan Coolidge (1835–1905)

Will

There is no chance, no destiny, no fate,
Can circumvent or hinder or control
The firm resolve of a determined soul.
Gifts count for nothing; will alone is great;
All things give way before it, soon or late.
What obstacle can stay the mighty force
Of the sea-seeking river in its course,
Or cause the ascending orb of day to wait?
Each well-born soul must win what it deserves.
Let the fool prate of luck. The fortunate
Is he whose earnest purpose never swerves,
Whose slightest action or inaction serves
The one great aim. Why, even Death stands still,
And waits an hour sometimes for such a will.

Ella Wheeler Wilcox (1850–1919)

Invictus

Out of the night that covers me,
  Black as the pit from pole to pole,
I thank whatever gods may be
  For my unconquerable soul.

In the fell clutch of circumstance
  I have not winced nor cried aloud.
Under the bludgeonings of chance
  My head is bloody, but unbowed.

Beyond this place of wrath and tears
  Looms but the Horror of the shade,
And yet the menace of the years
  Finds and shall find me unafraid.

It matters not how strait the gate,
  How charged with punishments the scroll,
I am the master of my fate,
  I am the captain of my soul.

W. E. Henley (1849–1903)

Ain't I a Woman?

That man over there say
   a woman needs to be helped into carriages
and lifted over ditches
   and to have the best place everywhere.
Nobody ever helped me into carriages
   or over mud puddles
      or gives me a best place ...

And ain't I a woman?
   Look at me!
Look at my arm!
   I have plowed and planted
and gathered into barns
   and no man could head me ...
And ain't I a woman?
   I could work as much
and eat as much as a man –
   when I could get to it –
and bear the lash as well,
   and ain't I a woman?
I have born thirteen children
   and seen most all sold into slavery
and when I cried out a mother's grief
   none but Jesus heard me ...
And ain't I a woman?
   That little man in black there say
a woman can't have as much rights as a man
   cause Christ wasn't a woman.
Where did your Christ come from?
   From God and a woman!

Man had nothing to do with him!
   If the first woman God ever made
was strong enough to turn the world
   upside down, all alone
together women ought to be able to turn it
   rightside up again.

> *Sojourner Truth and Erlene Stetson*
> *(1797–1883 and c.1949–)*

This, Too, Shall Pass Away

When some great sorrow like a mighty river,
Flows through your life with peace-destroying power,
And dearest things are swept from sight forever,
Say to your heart each trying hour:
    'This, too, shall pass away.'

When ceaseless toil has hushed your song of gladness,
And you have grown almost too tired to pray,
Let this truth banish from your heart its sadness,
And ease the burdens of each trying day:
    'This, too, shall pass away.'

When fortune smiles, and, full of mirth and pleasure,
The days are flitting by without a care,
Lest you should rest with only earthly treasure,
Let these few words their fullest import bear:
    'This, too, shall pass away.'

When earnest labor brings you fame and glory,
And all earth's noblest ones upon you smile,
Remember that life's longest, grandest story
Fills but a moment in earth's little while:
    'This, too, shall pass away.'

Lanta Wilson Smith (1856–1939)

'Hope' is the Thing with Feathers

'Hope' is the thing with feathers –
That perches in the soul –
And sings the tune without the words –
And never stops – at all –

And sweetest – in the Gale – is heard –
And sore must be the storm –
That could abash the little Bird
That kept so many warm –

I've heard it in the chillest land –
And on the strangest Sea –
Yet, never, in Extremity,
It asked a crumb – of Me.

Emily Dickinson (1830–1886)

Shut Not Your Doors to Me, Proud Libraries

Shut not your doors to me, proud libraries,
For that which was lacking among you all, yet needed
    most, I bring;
A book I have made for your dear sake, O soldiers,
And for you, O soul of man, and you, love of comrades;
The words of my book nothing, the life of it everything;
A book separate, not link'd with the rest, nor felt by
    the intellect;
But you will feel every word, O Libertad! arm'd
    Libertad!
It shall pass by the intellect to swim the sea, the air,
With joy with you, O soul of man.

Walt Whitman (1819–1892)

Courage

Courage is the price that Life exacts for granting peace.

The soul that knows it not knows no release
From little things:

Knows not the livid loneliness of fear,
Nor mountain heights where bitter joy can hear
The sound of wings.

How can life grant us boon of living, compensate
For dull gray ugliness and pregnant hate
Unless we dare

The soul's dominion? Each time we make a choice,
   we pay
With courage to behold the resistless day,
And count it fair.

Amelia Earhart (1897–1937)

The Call

From our low seat beside the fire
    Where we have dozed and dreamed and watched the glow
Or raked the ashes, stopping so
We scarcely saw the sun or rain
    Above, or looked much higher
Than this same quiet red or burned-out fire.
        To-night we heard a call,
        A rattle on the window-pane,
        A voice on the sharp air,
And felt a breath stirring our hair,
    A flame within us: Something swift and tall
Swept in and out and that was all.
Was it a bright or a dark angel? Who can know?
    It left no mark upon the snow,
        But suddenly it snapped the chain
        Unbarred, flung wide the door
        Which will not shut again;
And so we cannot sit here any more.

        We must arise and go:
        The world is cold without
        And dark and hedged about
With mystery and enmity and doubt,
        But we must go
        Though yet we do not know
Who called, or what marks we shall leave upon the snow.

Charlotte Mew (1869–1928)

A Pebble

Drop a pebble in the water: just a splash, and it is gone;
But there's half-a-hundred ripples circling on and on and on,
Spreading, spreading from the center, flowing on out to the sea.
And there is no way of telling where the end is going to be.

Drop a pebble in the water: in a minute you forget,
But there's little waves a-flowing, and there's ripples circling yet,
And those little waves a-flowing to a great big wave have grown;
You've disturbed a mighty river just by dropping in a stone.

Drop an unkind word, or careless: in a minute it is gone;
But there's half-a-hundred ripples circling on and on and on.
They keep spreading, spreading, spreading from the center as they go,
And there is no way to stop them, once you've started them to flow.

Drop an unkind word, or careless: in a minute you forget;
But there's little waves a-flowing, and there's ripples circling yet,

And perhaps in some sad heart a mighty wave of tears you've stirred,
And disturbed a life was happy ere you dropped that unkind word.

Drop a word of cheer and kindness: just a flash and it is gone;
But there's half-a-hundred ripples circling on and on and on,
Bearing hope and joy and comfort on each splashing, dashing wave
Till you wouldn't believe the volume of the one kind word you gave.

Drop a word of cheer and kindness: in a minute you forget;
But there's gladness still a-swelling, and there's joy circling yet,
And you've rolled a wave of comfort whose sweet music can be heard
Over miles and miles of water just by dropping one kind word.

James W. Foley (1874–1939)

from Henry V

This day is called the feast of Crispian:
He that outlives this day, and comes safe home,
Will stand a tip-toe when the day is named,
And rouse him at the name of Crispian.
He that shall live this day, and see old age,
Will yearly on the vigil feast his neighbours,
And say, 'To-morrow is Saint Crispian.'
Then will he strip his sleeve and show his scars,
And say, 'These wounds I had on Crispin's day.'
Old men forget; yet all shall be forgot,
But he'll remember with advantages
What feats he did that day. Then shall our names,
Familiar in his mouth as household words –
Harry the King, Bedford and Exeter,
Warwick and Talbot, Salisbury and Gloucester –
Be in their flowing cups freshly remember'd.
This story shall the good man teach his son;
And Crispin Crispian shall ne'er go by,
From this day to the ending of the world,
But we in it shall be remembered;
We few, we happy few, we band of brothers;
For he today that sheds his blood with me
Shall be my brother; be he ne'er so vile,
This day shall gentle his condition;
And gentlemen in England now a-bed
Shall think themselves accursed they were not here,
And hold their manhoods cheap whiles any speaks
That fought with us upon Saint Crispin's day.

William Shakespeare (1564–1616)

The New Colossus

Not like the brazen giant of Greek fame,
With conquering limbs astride from land to land;
Here at our sea-washed, sunset gates shall stand
A mighty woman with a torch, whose flame
Is the imprisoned lightning, and her name
Mother of Exiles. From her beacon-hand
Glows world-wide welcome; her mild eyes command
The air-bridged harbor that twin cities frame.
'Keep, ancient lands, your storied pomp!' cries she
With silent lips. 'Give me your tired, your poor,
Your huddled masses yearning to breathe free,
The wretched refuse of your teeming shore.
Send these, the homeless, tempest-tost to me,
I lift my lamp beside the golden door!'

Emma Lazarus (1849–1887)

The Gettysburg Address

Four score and seven years ago our fathers brought forth on this continent, a new nation, conceived in Liberty, and dedicated to the proposition that all men are created equal.

Now we are engaged in a great civil war, testing whether that nation, or any nation so conceived and so dedicated, can long endure. We are met on a great battlefield of that war. We have come to dedicate a portion of that field, as a final resting place for those who here gave their lives that that nation might live. It is altogether fitting and proper that we should do this.

But, in a larger sense, we can not dedicate – we can not consecrate – we can not hallow – this ground. The brave men, living and dead, who struggled here, have consecrated it, far above our poor power to add or detract. The world will little note, nor long remember what we say here, but it can never forget what they did here. It is for us the living, rather, to be dedicated here to the unfinished work which they who fought here have thus far so nobly advanced. It is rather for us to be here, dedicated to the great task remaining before us – that from these honored dead we take increased devotion to that cause for which they gave the last full measure of devotion – that we here highly resolve that these dead shall not have died in vain – that this nation, under God, shall have a new birth of freedom – and that government of the people, by the people, for the people, shall not perish from the earth.

Abraham Lincoln (1809–1865)

The Star-Spangled Banner

O say, can you see, by the dawn's early light,
What so proudly we hailed at the twilight's last
  gleaming?
Whose broad stripes and bright stars through the
  perilous fight,
O'er the ramparts we watched were so gallantly
  streaming;
And the rocket's red glare, the bombs bursting in air,
Gave proof through the night that our flag was still
  there;
O say, does that star-spangled banner yet wave
O'er the land of the free, and the home of the brave?

On the shore dimly seen through the mists of the deep,
Where the foe's haughty host in dread silence reposes,
What is that which the breeze, o'er the towering steep,
As it fitfully blows, now conceals, now discloses?
Now it catches the gleam of the morning's first beam,
In full glory reflected now shines on the stream;
'Tis the star-spangled banner; O long may it wave
O'er the land of the free, and the home of the brave!

And where is that band who so vauntingly swore
That the havoc of war and the battle's confusion
A home and a country should leave us no more?
Their blood has washed out their foul footsteps'
  pollution.
No refuge could save the hireling and slave,
From the terror of flight and the gloom of the grave;
And the star-spangled banner in triumph doth wave
O'er the land of the free, and the home of the brave!

O! thus be it ever, when freemen shall stand
Between their loved homes and the war's desolation!
Blest with victory and peace, may the heav'n-rescued
   land
Praise the power that hath made and preserved us
   a nation.
Then conquer we must, for our cause it is just.
And this be our motto – 'In God is our trust';
And the star-spangled banner in triumph shall wave
O'er the land of the free, and the home of the brave.

Francis Scott Key (1779–1843)

I Hear America Singing

I hear America singing, the varied carols I hear,
Those of mechanics, each one singing his as it should
  be blithe and strong,
The carpenter singing his as he measures his plank
  or beam,
The mason singing his as he makes ready for work, or
  leaves off work,
The boatman singing what belongs to him in his boat,
  the deckhand singing on the steamboat deck,
The shoemaker singing as he sits on his bench, the
  hatter singing as he stands,
The wood-cutter's song, the ploughboy's on his way
  in the morning, or at noon intermission or at
  sundown,
The delicious singing of the mother, or of the young
  wife at work, or of the girl sewing or washing,
Each singing what belongs to him or her and to
  none else,
The day what belongs to the day – at night the party
  of young fellows, robust, friendly,
Singing with open mouths their strong melodious songs.

Walt Whitman (1819–1892)

No Coward Soul Is Mine

No coward soul is mine,
No trembler in the world's storm-troubled sphere:
I see Heaven's glories shine,
And faith shines equal, arming me from Fear.

O God within my breast,
Almighty, ever-present Deity!
Life – that in me hast rest,
As I – Undying Life – have power in Thee!

Vain are the thousand creeds
That move men's hearts, unutterably vain;
Worthless as withered weeds
Or idlest froth amid the boundless main,

To waken doubt in one
Holding so fast by Thine infinity;
So surely anchored on
The steadfast rock of immortality.

With wide-embracing love
Thy Spirit animates eternal years,
Pervades and broods above,
Changes, sustains, dissolves, creates and rears

Though Earth and moon were gone,
And suns and universes ceased to be,
And Thou wert left alone,
Every Existence would exist in Thee.

There is not room for Death,
Nor atom that his might could render void:
Thou – Thou art Being and Breath,
And what Thou art may never be destroyed.

Emily Brontë (1818–1848)

A Summing Up

I have lived and I have loved;
I have waked and I have slept;
I have sung and I have danced;
I have smiled and I have wept;
I have won and wasted treasure;
I have had my fill of pleasure;
And all these things were weariness,
And some of them were dreariness,
And all these things, but two things,
Were emptiness and pain:
And Love – it was the best of them;
And Sleep – worth all the rest of them.

Charles Mackay (1814–1889)

FRIENDSHIP IS LOVE
WITHOUT HIS WINGS

L'amitié Est L'amour Sans Ailes

Why should my anxious breast repine,
   Because my youth is fled?
Days of delight may still be mine;
   Affection is not dead.
In tracing back the years of youth,
One firm record, one lasting truth
   Celestial consolation brings;
Bear it, ye breezes, to the seat,
Where first my heart responsive beat, –
   'Friendship is Love without his wings!'

Through few, but deeply chequer'd years,
   What moments have been mine!
Now half obscured by clouds of tears,
   Now bright in rays divine;
Howe'er my future doom be cast,
My soul, enraptured with the past,
   To one idea fondly clings;
Friendship! that thought is all thine own,
Worth worlds of bliss, that thought alone –
   'Friendship is Love without his Wings!'

Where yonder yew-trees lightly wave
   Their branches on the gale,
Unheeded heaves a simple grave,
   Which tells the common tale;
Round this unconcious schoolboys stray,
Till the dull knell of childish play
   From yonder studious mansion rings;
But here, whene'er my footsteps move,
My silent tears too plainly prove
   'Friendship is Love without his wings!'

Oh Love, before thy glowing shrine
  My early vows were paid;
My hopes, my dreams, my heart was thine,
  But these are now decay'd;
For thine are pinions like the wind,
No trace of thee remains behind,
  Except, alas! thy jealous stings.
Away, away! delusive power,
Thou shalt not haunt my coming hour;
  Unless, indeed, without thy wings.

Seat of my youth! thy distant spire
  Recalls each scene of joy;
My bosom glows with former fire, –
  In mind again a boy.
Thy grove of elms, thy verdant hill,
Thy every path delights me still,
  Each flower a double fragrance flings;
Again, as once, in converse gay,
Each dear associate seems to say,
  'Friendship is Love without his wings!'

My Lycus! wherefore dost thou weep?
  Thy falling tears restrain;
Affection for a time may sleep,
  But, oh, 'twill wake again.
Think, think, my friend, when next we meet,
Our long-wish'd interview, how sweet!
  From this my hope of rapture springs;
While youthful hearts thus fondly swell,
Absence, my friend, can only tell,
  'Friendship is Love without his wings!'

In one, and one alone deceiv'd,
   Did I my error mourn?
No – from oppressive bonds reliev'd,
   I left the wretch to scorn.
I turn'd to those my childhood knew,
With feelings warm, with bosoms true,
   Twin'd with my heart's according strings,
And till those vital chords shall break,
For none but these my breast shall wake
   'Friendship, the power deprived of wings!'

Ye few! my soul, my life is yours,
   My memory and my hope,
Your worth a lasting love insures,
   Unfetter'd in its scope;
From smooth deceit and terror sprung,
With aspect fair and honey'd tongue,
   Let Adulation wait on kings;
With joy elate, by snares beset,
We, we, my friends, can ne'er forget,
   'Friendship is Love without his wings!'

Fictions and dreams inspire the bard
   Who rolls the epic song;
Friendship and truth be my reward –
   To me no bays belong;
If laurell'd Fame but dwells with lies,
Me the Enchantress ever flies,
   Whose heart and not whose fancy sings;
Simple and young, I dare not feign;
Mine be the rude yet heartfelt strain,
   'Friendship is Love without his wings!'

Lord Byron (1788–1824)

Outwitted

He drew a circle that shut me out –
Heretic, rebel, a thing to flout.
But Love and I had the wit to win:
We drew a circle that took him in!

Edwin Markham (1852–1940)

We Two Boys Together Clinging

We two boys together clinging,
One the other never leaving,
Up and down the roads going, North and South
  excursions making,
Power enjoying, elbows stretching, fingers clutching,
Arm'd and fearless, eating, drinking, sleeping, loving,
No law less than ourselves owning, sailing, soldiering,
  thieving, threatening,
Misers, menials, priests alarming, air breathing, water
  drinking, on the turf or the sea-beach dancing,
Cities wrenching, ease scorning, statutes mocking,
  feebleness chasing,
Fulfilling our foray.

Walt Whitman (1819–1892)

Friendship

Oh, the comfort –
the inexpressible comfort of feeling *safe* with a person –
having neither to weigh thoughts nor measure words,
but pouring them all right out,
just as they are,
chaff and grain together;
certain that a faithful hand will take and sift them,
keep what is worth keeping,
and then with the breath of kindness blow the rest away.

Dinah Maria Craik (1826–1887)

Forbearance

Hast thou named all the birds without a gun?
Loved the wood-rose, and left it on its stalk?
At rich men's tables eaten bread and pulse?
Unarmed, faced danger with a heart of trust?
And loved so well a high behavior,
In man or maid, that thou from speech refrained,
Nobility more nobly to repay?
O, be my friend, and teach me to be thine!

Ralph Waldo Emerson (1803–1882)

Friendship

Like a quetzal plume, a fragrant flower,
friendship sparkles:
like heron plumes, it weaves itself into finery.
Our song is a bird calling out like a jingle:
how beautiful you make it sound!
Here, among flowers that enclose us,
among flowery boughs you are singing.

Aztec, Traditional

Travelling

This is the spot: – how mildly does the sun
Shine in between the fading leaves! the air
In the habitual silence of this wood
Is more than silent: and this bed of heath,
Where shall we find so sweet a resting-place?
Come! – let me see thee sink into a dream
Of quiet thoughts, – protracted till thine eye
Be calm as water when the winds are gone
And no one can tell whither – my sweet friend!
We two have had such happy hours together
That my heart melts in me to think of it.

William Wordsworth (1770–1850)

Love and Friendship

Love is like the wild rose-briar,
Friendship like the holly-tree –
The holly is dark when the rose-briar blooms
But which will bloom most constantly?

The wild rose-briar is sweet in spring,
Its summer blossoms scent the air;
Yet wait till winter comes again
And who will call the wild-briar fair?

Then scorn the silly rose-wreath now
And deck thee with the holly's sheen,
That when December blights thy brow
He still may leave thy garland green.

Emily Brontë (1818–1848)

New Friends and Old Friends

Make new friends, but keep the old;
Those are silver, these are gold.
New-made friendships, like new wine,
Age will mellow and refine.
Friendships that have stood the test –
Time and change – are surely best;
Brow may wrinkle, hair grow gray,
Friendship never knows decay.
For 'mid old friends, tried and true,
Once more we our youth renew.
But old friends, alas! may die,
New friends must their place supply.
Cherish friendship in your breast –
New is good, but old is best;
Make new friends, but keep the old;
Those are silver, these are gold.

Joseph Parry (1841–1903)

HE WISHES FOR
THE CLOTHS OF HEAVEN

He Wishes for the Cloths of Heaven

Had I the heavens' embroidered cloths,
Enwrought with golden and silver light,
The blue and the dim and the dark cloths
Of night and light and the half-light,
I would spread the cloths under your feet:
But I, being poor, have only my dreams;
I have spread my dreams under your feet;
Tread softly because you tread on my dreams.

W. B. Yeats (1865–1939)

How Do I Love Thee?

How do I love thee? Let me count the ways,
I love thee to the depth and breadth and height
My soul can reach, when feeling out of sight
For the ends of Being and ideal Grace.

I love thee to the level of everyday's
Most quiet need, by sun and candlelight.
I love thee freely, as men strive for Right;
I love thee purely, as they turn from Praise.

I love thee with the passion put to use
In my old griefs, and with my childhood's faith.
I love thee with a love I seemed to lose

With my lost saints – I love thee with the breath,
Smiles, tears, of all my life! – and, if God choose
I shall but love thee better after death.

Elizabeth Barrett Browning (1806–1861)

Sonnet 18

Shall I compare thee to a summer's day?
Thou art more lovely and more temperate:
Rough winds do shake the darling buds of May,
And summer's lease hath all too short a date:
Sometime too hot the eye of heaven shines,
And often is his gold complexion dimm'd;
And every fair from fair sometime declines,
By chance or nature's changing course untrimm'd;
But thy eternal summer shall not fade,
Nor lose possession of that fair thou ow'st;
Nor shall Death brag thou wander'st in his shade,
When in eternal lines to time thou grow'st:
   So long as men can breathe, or eyes can see,
   So long lives this, and this gives life to thee.

William Shakespeare (1564–1616)

Meeting at Night

The grey sea and the long black land;
And the yellow half-moon large and low;
And the startled little waves that leap
In fiery ringlets from their sleep,
As I gain the cove with pushing prow,
And quench its speed i' the slushy sand.

Then a mile of warm sea-scented beach;
Three fields to cross till a farm appears;
A tap at the pane, the quick sharp scratch
And blue spurt of a lighted match,
And a voice less loud, through joys and fears,
Than the two hearts beating each to each!

Robert Browning (1812–1889)

To a Friend

I ask but one thing of you, only one,
That you will always be my dream of you;
That never shall I wake to find untrue
All this I have believed and rested on,
Forever vanished, like a vision gone
Out into the night. Alas, how few
There are who strike in us a chord we knew
Existed, but so seldom heard its tone
We tremble at the half-forgotten sound.
The world is full of rude awakenings
And heaven-born castles shattered to the ground,
Yet still our human longing vainly clings
To a belief in beauty through all wrongs.
O stay your hand, and leave my heart its songs!

Amy Lowell (1874–1925)

A Birthday

My heart is like a singing bird,
  Whose nest is in a watered shoot;
My heart is like an apple-tree
  Whose boughs are bent with thick-set fruit;
My heart is like a rainbow shell
  That paddles in a halcyon sea;
My heart is gladder than all these
  Because my love is come to me.

Raise me a dais of silk and down;
  Hang it with vair and purple dyes;
Carve it in doves and pomegranates,
  And peacocks with a hundred eyes;
Work it in gold and silver grapes,
  In leaves and silver fleurs-de-lys;
Because the birthday of my life
  Is come, my love is come to me.

Christina Rossetti (1830–1894)

Upon Julia's Clothes

When as in silks my Julia goes,
Then, then (me thinks) how sweetly flowes
That liquefaction of her clothes.

Next, when I cast mine eyes and see
That brave Vibration each way free;
O how that glittering taketh me!

Robert Herrick (1591–1674)

Rose-cheeked Laura

Rose-cheeked Laura, come,
Sing thou smoothly with thy beauties
Silent music, either other
    Sweetly gracing.

Lovely forms do flow
From consent divinely framèd;
Heaven is music, and thy beauty's
    Birth is heavenly.

These dull notes we sing
Discords need for helps to grace them;
Only beauty purely loving
    Knows no discord,

But still moves delight,
Like clear springs renewed by flowing,
Ever perfect, ever in them-
    selves eternal.

Thomas Campion (1567–1620)

In an Artist's Studio

One face looks out from all his canvases,
  One selfsame figure sits or walks or leans:
  We found her hidden just behind those screens,
That mirror gave back all her loveliness.
A queen in opal or in ruby dress,
  A nameless girl in freshest summer-greens,
  A saint, an angel – every canvas means
The same one meaning, neither more nor less.
He feeds upon her face by day and night,
  And she with true kind eyes looks back on him,
Fair as the moon and joyful as the light:
  Not wan with waiting, not with sorrow dim;
Not as she is, but was when hope shone bright;
  Not as she is, but as she fills his dream.

Christina Rossetti (1830–1894)

'It was a lover and his lass'

It was a lover and his lass
  With a hey and a ho, and a hey nonino!
That o'er the green corn-field did pass
In the spring time, the only pretty ring time,
When birds do sing hey ding a ding:
  Sweet lovers love the Spring.

Between the acres of the rye
These pretty country folks would lie:
This carol they began that hour,
How that life was but a flower:

And therefore take the present time
  With a hey and a ho and a hey nonino!
For love is crownéd with the prime
In spring time, the only pretty ring time,
When birds do sing hey ding a ding:
  Sweet lovers love the Spring.

William Shakespeare (1564–1616)

Love Lightly Pleased

Let fair or foul my mistress be,
Or low, or tall, she pleaseth me;
Or let her walk, or stand, or sit,
The posture her's, I'm pleased with it;
Or let her tongue be still, or stir,
Graceful is every thing from her;
Or let her grant, or else deny,
My love will fit each history.

Robert Herrick (1591–1674)

Invitation to Love

Come when the nights are bright with stars
Or come when the moon is mellow;
Come when the sun his golden bars
Drops on the hay-field yellow.
Come in the twilight soft and gray,
Come in the night or come in the day,
Come, O love, whene'er you may,
And you are welcome, welcome.

You are sweet, O Love, dear Love,
You are soft as the nesting dove.
Come to my heart and bring it to rest
As the bird flies home to its welcome nest.

Come when my heart is full of grief
Or when my heart is merry;
Come with the falling of the leaf
Or with the redd'ning cherry.
Come when the year's first blossom blows,
Come when the summer gleams and glows,
Come with the winter's drifting snows,
And you are welcome, welcome.

Paul Laurence Dunbar (1876–1906)

from Paradise Lost

Here, Eve speaks to Adam.

With thee conversing I forget all time,
All seasons and their change, all please alike.
Sweet is the breath of morn, her rising sweet,
With charm of earliest birds; pleasant the sun
When first on this delightful land he spreads
His orient beams, on herb, tree, fruit, and flower,
Glistring with dew; fragrant the fertile earth
After soft showers; and sweet the coming on
Of grateful evening mild, then silent night
With this her solemn bird and this fair moon,
And these the gems of heav'n, her starry train:
But neither breath of morn when she ascends
With charm of earliest birds, nor rising sun
On this delightful land, nor herb, fruit, flower,
Glistring with dew, nor fragrance after showers,
Nor grateful evening mild, nor silent night
With this her solemn bird, nor walk by moon,
Or glittering starlight without thee is sweet.

John Milton (1608–1674)

Fulfillment

There is no happier life
   But in a wife;
The comforts are so sweet
   When two do meet.
'Tis plenty, peace, a calm
   Like dropping balm;
Love's weather is so fair,
   Like perfumed air.
Each word such pleasure brings
   Like soft-touched strings;
Love's passion moves the heart
   On either part;
Such harmony together,
   So pleased in either.
No discords; concords still;
   Sealed with one will.
By love, God made man one,
   Yet not alone.
Like stamps of king and queen
   It may be seen:
Two figures on one coin,
   So do they join,
Only they not embrace.
   We, face to face.

William Cavendish (1592–1676)

from Sonnets from the Portuguese

I thank all who have loved me in their hearts,
With thanks and love from mine. Deep thanks to all
Who paused a little near the prison-wall
To hear my music in its louder parts
Ere they went onward, each one to the mart's
Or temple's occupation, beyond call.
But thou, who, in my voice's sink and fall
When the sob took it, thy divinest Art's
Own instrument didst drop down at thy foot
To hearken what I said between my tears, ...
Instruct me how to thank thee! Oh, to shoot
My soul's full meaning into future years,
That they should lend it utterance, and salute
Love that endures, from Life that disappears!

Elizabeth Barrett Browning (1806–1861)

Camomile Tea

Outside the sky is light with stars;
There's a hollow roaring from the sea.
And, alas! for the little almond flowers,
The wind is shaking the almond tree.

How little I thought, a year ago,
In the horrible cottage upon the Lee,
That he and I should be sitting so
And sipping a cup of camomile tea.

Light as feathers the witches fly,
The horn of the moon is plain to see;
By a firefly under a jonquil flower
A goblin toasts a bumble-bee.

We might be fifty, we might be five,
So snug, so compact, so wise are we!
Under the kitchen-table leg
My knee is pressing against his knee.

Katherine Mansfield (1888–1923)

When I Heard at the Close of the Day

When I heard at the close of the day how my name
    had been receiv'd with plaudits in the capitol, still
    it was not a happy night for me that follow'd,
And else when I carous'd, or when my plans were
    accomplish'd, still I was not happy. But the day
    when I rose at dawn from the bed of perfect health,
    refresh'd, singing, inhaling the ripe breath of autumn,
When I saw the full moon in the west grow pale and
    disappear in the morning light,
When I wander'd alone over the beach, and
    undressing bathed, laughing with the cool waters,
    and saw the sun rise,
And when I thought how my dear friend my lover was
    on his way coming, O then I was happy,
O then each breath tasted sweeter, and all that day
    my food nourish'd me more, and the beautiful day
    pass'd well,
And the next came with equal joy, and with the next
    at evening came my friend,
And that night while all was still I heard the waters
    roll slowly continually up the shores,
I heard the hissing rustle of the liquid and sands as
    directed to me whispering to congratulate me,
For the one I love most lay sleeping by me under the
    same cover in the cool night,
In the stillness in the autumn moonbeams his face
    was inclined toward me,
And his arm lay lightly around my breast – and that
    night I was happy.

Walt Whitman (1819–1892)

Song

When as the rye reach to the chin,
  And chopcherry, chopcherry ripe within,
Strawberries swimming in the cream,
And school-boys playing in the stream;
  Then O, then O, then O my true love said,
    Till that time come again,
    She could not live a maid.

George Peele (c.1558–1597)

To Althea, from Prison

When Love with unconfinèd wings
   Hovers within my gates;
And my divine Althea brings
   To whisper at the grates;
When I lie tangled in her hair,
   And fettered to her eye;
The Gods that wanton in the air
   Know no such liberty.

When flowing cups run swiftly round
   With no allaying Thames,
Our careless heads with roses bound
   Our hearts with loyal flames;
When thirsty grief in wine we steep,
   When healths and draughts go free,
Fishes that tipple in the deep
   Know no such liberty.

When, like committed linnets, I
   With shriller throat shall sing
The sweetness, mercy, majesty,
   And glories of my King;
When I shall voice aloud how good
   He is, how great should be,
Enlargèd winds that curl the flood
   Know no such liberty.

Stone walls do not a prison make,
   Nor iron bars a cage;

Minds innocent and quiet take
  That for an hermitage;
If I have freedom in my love,
  And in my soul am free;
Angels alone that soar above
  Enjoy such liberty.

Richard Lovelace (c. 1618–1657)

A Decade

When you came, you were like red wine and honey,
And the taste of you burnt my mouth with its sweetness.
Now you are like morning bread,
Smooth and pleasant.
I hardly taste you at all for I know your savour,
But I am completely nourished.

Amy Lowell (1874–1925)

THE SHAPE OF A GOOD GREYHOUND

The Shape of a Good Greyhound

A head like a snake,
a neck like a drake.
A back like a beam,
a belly like a bream.
A foot like a cat,
a tail like a rat.

Anon.

The Lurcher

Forth goes the woodman, leaving unconcerned
The cheerful haunts of men to wield the axe
And drive the wedge in yonder forest drear,
From morn to eve his solitary task.
Shaggy and lean and shrewd, with pointed ears
And tail cropped short, half-lurcher and half-cur,
His dog attends him. Close behind his heel
Now creeps he slow, and now with many a frisk
Wide scampering, snatches up the drifted snow
With ivory teeth, or ploughs it with his snout;
Then shakes his powder'd coat, and barks for joy.

William Cowper (1731–1800)

Dog

You little friend, your nose is ready; you sniff,
Asking for that expected walk,
(Your nostrils full of the happy rabbit-whiff)
And almost talk.

And so the moment becomes a moving force;
Coats glide down from their pegs in the humble dark;
The sticks grow live to the stride of their vagrant course.
You scamper the stairs,
Your body informed with the scent and the track and
    the mark
Of stoats and weasels, moles and badgers and hares.

We are going OUT. You know the pitch of the word,
Probing the tone of thought as it comes through fog
And reaches by devious means (half-smelt, half-heard)
The four-legged brain of a walk-ecstatic dog.

Out in the garden your head is already low.
(Can you smell the rose? Ah, no.)
But your limbs can draw
Life from the earth through the touch of your padded
    paw.

Now, sending a little look to us behind,
Who follow slowly the track of your lovely play,
You carry our bodies forward away from mind
Into the light and fun of your useless day.

*

Thus, for your walk, we took ourselves, and went
Out by the hedge and the tree to the open ground.
You ran, in delightful strata of wafted scent,
Over the hill without seeing the view;
Beauty is smell upon primitive smell to you:
To you, as to us, it is distant and rarely found.

Home ... and further joy will be surely there:
Supper waiting full of the taste of bone.
You throw up your nose again, and sniff, and stare
For the rapture known

Of the quick wild gorge of food and the still lie-down
While your people talk above you in the light
Of candles, and your dreams will merge and drown
Into the bed-delicious hours of night.

Harold Monro (1879–1932)

The Windhover

To Christ our Lord

I caught this morning morning's minion, king-
    dom of daylight's dauphin, dapple-dawn-drawn
        Falcon, in his riding
    Of the rolling level underneath him steady air,
        and striding
High there, how he rung upon the rein of a
    wimpling wing
In his ecstasy! then off, off forth on swing,
    As a skate's heel sweeps smooth on a bow-bend:
        the hurl and gliding
    Rebuffed the big wind. My heart in hiding
Stirred for a bird, – the achieve of, the mastery of the
    thing!

Brute beauty and valour and act, oh, air, pride,
    plume, here
        Buckle! AND the fire that breaks from thee then,
        a billion
Times told lovelier, more dangerous, O my chevalier!

    No wonder of it: shéer plód makes plough down
        sillion
Shine, and blue-bleak embers, ah my dear,
    Fall, gall themselves, and gash gold-vermilion.

Gerard Manley Hopkins (1844–1889)

A Winter Bluejay

Crisply the bright snow whispered,
Crunching beneath our feet;
Behind us as we walked along the parkway,
Our shadows danced
Fantastic shapes in vivid blue.
Across the lake the skaters
Flew to and fro,
With sharp turns weaving
A frail invisible net.
In ecstasy the earth
Drank the silver sunlight;
In ecstasy the skaters
Drank the wine of speed;
In ecstasy we laughed
Drinking the wine of love.
Had not the music of our joy
Sounded its highest note?
But no,
For suddenly, with lifted eyes you said,
'Oh look!'
There, on the black bough of a snow-flecked maple,
Fearless and gay as our love,
A bluejay cocked his crest!
Oh, who can tell the range of joy
Or set the bounds of beauty?

Sara Teasdale (1884–1933)

from To a Skylark

Hail to thee, blithe Spirit!
Bird thou never wert,
That from heaven or near it,
Pourest thy full heart
In profuse strains of unpremeditated art.

Higher still and higher
From the earth thou springest
Like a cloud of fire;
The blue deep thou wingest,
And singing still doth soar, and soaring ever singest.

Percy Bysshe Shelley (1792–1822)

'Pack, clouds, away, and welcome day'

Pack, clouds, away, and welcome day,
  With night we banish sorrow;
Sweet air blow soft, mount larks aloft
  To give my Love good-morrow!
Wings from the wind to please her mind
  Notes from the lark I'll borrow;
Bird, prune thy wing, nightingale sing,
  To give my Love good-morrow;
    To give my Love good-morrow
    Notes from them both I'll borrow.

Wake from thy nest, Robin-red-breast,
  Sing, birds, in every furrow;
And from each hill, let music shrill
  Give my fair Love good-morrow!
Blackbird and thrush in every bush,
  Stare, linnet, and cock-sparrow!
You pretty elves, amongst yourselves
  Sing my fair Love good-morrow;
    To give my Love good-morrow
    Sing, birds, in every furrow!

Thomas Heywood (c. 1574–1641)

from Jubilate Agno
(A Poem from Bedlam)

For I will consider my cat Jeoffry.
For he is the servant of the living God, duly and daily serving him.
For at the first glance of the glory of God in the East he worships in his way.
For this is done by wreathing his body seven times round with elegant quickness.
For when he leaps up to catch the musk, which is the blessing of God upon his prayer.
For he rolls upon prank to work it in.
For having done duty and received blessing he begins to consider himself.
For this he performs in ten degrees.
For first he looks upon his fore-paws to see if they are clean.
For secondly he kicks up behind to clear away there.
For thirdly he works it upon stretch with the fore-paws extended.
For fourthly he sharpens his paws by wood.
For fifthly he washes himself.
For sixthly he rolls upon wash.
For seventhly he fleas himself, that he may not be interrupted upon the beat.
For eighthly he rubs himself against a post.
For ninthly he looks up for his instructions.
For tenthly he goes in quest of food.
For having consider'd God and himself he will consider his neighbour.
For if he meets another cat he will kiss her in kindness.

For when he takes his prey he plays with it to give it
    a chance.
For one mouse in seven escapes by his dallying.
For when his day's work is done his business more
    properly begins.
For he keeps the Lord's watch in the night against the
    adversary.
For he counteracts the powers of darkness by his
    electrical skin and glaring eyes.
For he counteracts the Devil, who is death, by brisking
    about the life.
For in his morning orisons he loves the sun and the
    sun loves him.
For he is of the tribe of Tiger.
For the Cherub Cat is a term of the Angel Tiger.
For he has the subtlety and hissing of a serpent, which
    in goodness he suppresses.
For he will not do destruction, if he is well-fed, neither
    will he spit without provocation.
For he purrs in thankfulness, when God tells him he's
    a good Cat.
For he is an instrument for the children to learn
    benevolence upon.
For every house is incompleat without him & a
    blessing is lacking in the Spirit.
For the Lord commanded Moses concerning the cats
    at the departure of the Children of Israel
    from Egypt.
For every family had one cat at least in the bag.
For the English cats are the best in Europe.
For he is the cleanest in the use of his fore-paws of any
    quadrupeds.
For the dexterity of his defence is an instance of the
    love of God to him exceedingly.

For he is the quickest to his mark of any creature.
For he is tenacious of his point.
For he is a mixture of gravity and waggery.
For he knows that God is his Saviour.
For there is nothing sweeter than his peace when at rest.
For there is nothing brisker than his life when in motion.
For he is of the Lord's poor and so indeed is he called by benevolence perpetually – Poor Jeoffry! poor Jeoffry! the rat has bit thy throat.
For I bless the name of the Lord Jesus that Jeoffry is better.
For the divine spirit comes about his body to sustain it in compleat cat.
For his tongue is exceeding pure so that it has in purity what it wants in musick.
For he is docile and can learn certain things.
For he can set up with gravity which is patience upon approbation.
For he can fetch and carry, which is patience in employment.
For he can jump over a stick which is patience upon proof positive.
For he can spraggle upon waggle at the word of command.
For he can jump from an eminence into his master's bosom.
For he can catch the cork and toss it again.
For he is hated by the hypocrite and miser.
For the former is afraid of detection.
For the latter refuses the charge.
For he camels his back to bear the first motion of business.
For he is good to think on, if a man would express himself neatly.

For he made a great figure in Egypt for his signal
   services.
For he killed the Icneumon-rat very pernicious by land.
For his ears are so acute that they sting again.
For from this proceeds the passing quickness of
   his attention.
For by stroaking of him I have found out electricity.
For I perceived God's light about him both wax
   and fire.
For the Electrical fire is the spiritual substance, which
   God sends from heaven to sustain the bodies both
   of man and beast.
For God has blessed him in the variety of his
   movements.
For, tho he cannot fly, he is an excellent clamberer.
For his motions upon the face of the earth are more
   than any other quadrupeds.
For he can tread to all the measures upon the musick.
For he can swim for life.
For he can creep.

Christopher Smart (1722–1771)

Pangur Bán

I and Pangur Bán, my cat,
'Tis a like task we are at;
Hunting mice is his delight,
Hunting words I sit all night.

Better far than praise of men
'Tis to sit with book and pen;
Pangur bears me no ill-will,
He too plies his simple skill.

'Tis a merry thing to see
At our tasks how glad are we,
When at home we sit and find
Entertainment to our mind.

Oftentimes a mouse will stray
In the hero Pangur's way;
Oftentimes my keen thought set
Takes a meaning in its net.

'Gainst the wall he sets his eye
Full and fierce and sharp and sly;
'Gainst the wall of knowledge I
All my little wisdom try.

When a mouse darts from its den,
O how glad is Pangur then!
O what gladness do I prove
When I solve the doubts I love!

So in peace our tasks we ply,
Pangur Bán, my cat, and I;
In our arts we find our bliss,
I have mine and he has his.

Practice every day has made
Pangur perfect in his trade;
I get wisdom day and night
Turning darkness into light.

Anon. tr. Robin Flower
(1881–1946)

The Owl and the Pussycat

The Owl and the Pussy-cat went to sea
  In a beautiful pea-green boat,
They took some honey, and plenty of money,
  Wrapped up in a five-pound note.
The Owl looked up to the stars above,
  And sang to a small guitar,
'O lovely Pussy! O Pussy, my love,
  What a beautiful Pussy you are,
    You are,
    You are!
What a beautiful Pussy you are!'

Pussy said to the Owl, 'You elegant fowl!
  How charmingly sweet you sing!
O let us be married! too long we have tarried:
  But what shall we do for a ring?'
They sailed away, for a year and a day,
  To the land where the Bong-tree grows
And there in a wood a Piggy-wig stood
  With a ring at the end of his nose,
    His nose,
    His nose,
With a ring at the end of his nose.

'Dear Pig, are you willing to sell for one shilling
  Your ring?' Said the Piggy, 'I will.'
So they took it away, and were married next day
  By the Turkey who lives on the hill.

They dined on mince, and slices of quince,
   Which they ate with a runcible spoon;
And hand in hand, on the edge of the sand,
   They danced by the light of the moon,
      The moon,
      The moon,
They danced by the light of the moon.

Edward Lear (1812–1888)

Seal Lullaby

Oh! hush thee, my baby, the night is behind us,
   And black are the waters that sparkled so green.
The moon, o'er the combers, looks downward to find us
   At rest in the hollows that rustle between.
Where billow meets billow, there soft be thy pillow;
   Ah, weary wee flipperling, curl at thy ease!
The storm shall not wake thee, nor shark overtake thee,
   Asleep in the arms of the slow-swinging seas.

Rudyard Kipling (1865–1936)

Index of Poets

Addison, Joseph 92
Alford, Henry 44
Anon. 5, 9, 12, 31, 41, 161, 173
Aztec, Traditional 130

Blake, William 14, 25, 59
Book of Ecclesiastes 15
Brontë, Emily 75, 117, 132
Browning, Elizabeth Barrett 138, 151
Browning, Robert 63, 140
Burns, Robert 53
Byron, Lord 123

Campion, Thomas 144
Cavendish, William 150
Charles I 6
Clare, John 80, 88
Clough, Arthur Hugh 97
Converse, Harriet Maxwell 42
Coolidge, Susan 99
Cotton, Charles 90
Cowper, William 162
Craik, Dinah Maria 128

Davies, W. H. 7, 62, 64
Dekker, Thomas 74
Dickinson, Emily 61, 78, 105
Donne, John 67
Drinkwater, John 84
Dryden, John 4

Index of Poets

Dunbar, Paul Laurence   148
Dyer, Sir Edward   22

Earhart, Amelia   107
Ehrmann, Max   47
Emerson, Ralph Waldo   40, 89, 129

Flower, Robin   173
Foley, James W.   109

Gould, Elizabeth   17

Henley, W. E.   101
Herbert, George   28
Herrick, Robert   57, 143, 147
Heywood, Thomas   168
Holtby, Winifred   54
Hopkins, Gerard Manley   35, 94, 165

Iroquois, Traditional   42, 49

Keats, John   16, 24, 86
Key, Francis Scott   114
Kingsley, Charles   26
Kipling, Rudyard   10, 177

Lazarus, Emma   112
Lear, Edward   175
Lincoln, Abraham   113
Lovelace, Richard   155
Lowell, Amy   141, 157

Mackay, Charles   119
Magee Jr, John Gillespie   8

Index of Poets

Mansfield, Katherine 152
Markham, Edwin 126
Mew, Charlotte 108
Milton, John 149
Monro, Harold 163

Newton, John 36

Parry, Joseph 133
Patmore, Coventry 81
Peele, George 154
Pope, Alexander 19

Raleigh, Sir Walter 51
Rossetti, Christina 13, 70, 142, 145
Runner, Olive 98

Sarum Missal 37
Service of the Orthodox Synagogue for the Festival of Tabernacles 50
Shakespeare, William 77, 79, 111, 139, 146
Shelley, Percy Bysshe 20, 167
Smart, Christopher 66, 169
Smith, Lanta Wilson 104
St Francis of Assisi 38
Stevenson, Robert Louis 3

Tagore, Rabindranath 52
Teasdale, Sara 65, 166
Tennyson, Alfred, Lord 73
Thomas, Edward 69
Truth, Sojourner and Stetson, Erlene 102

Index of Poets

Vaughan, Henry 27

Whitman, Walt 30, 39, 106, 116, 127, 153
Whittier, John Greenleaf 85
Wilcox, Ella Wheeler 100
Willis, Wallace 46
Wordsworth, William 60, 72, 82, 83, 93, 131

Yeats, W. B. 58, 76, 137

Index of Titles

A Birthday   142
A Decade   157
A Dumb Friend   70
A Farewell   26
A Greeting   64
A Little Health   31
A Pebble   109
A Summing Up   119
A Vision   27
A Winter Bluejay   166
Adoration   66
African Canticle   41
Ain't I a Woman?   102
Amazing Grace   36

Camomile Tea   152
Careless Rambles   80
Composed Upon Westminster Bridge,
   September 3, 1802   83
Courage   107

Desiderata   47
Dog   163

Epitaph   54
Eternity   25
Evening Quatrains   90

Father, We Thank Thee   40
February Twilight   65
Forbearance   129

Index of Titles

Freedom 98
Friendship 128
Friendship 130
from A Midsummer Night's Dream 79
from Auguries of Innocence 14
from Endymion 16
from Henry V 111
from His Pilgrimage 51
from Jubilate Agno 169
from Paradise Lost 149
from Pippa Passes 63
from Sonnets from the Portuguese 151
from To a Skylark 167
Fulfillment 150

God Be In My Head 37
God's Grandeur 94
Gratefulnesse 28

Happy the Man 4
Happy Thought 3
Harvest Home 44
Harvest Hymn 85
He Wishes for the Cloths of Heaven 137
High Flight 8
'Hope' is the Thing with Feathers 105
How Do I Love Thee? 138
Hurt No Living Thing 13

I Hear America Singing 116
I Wandered Lonely as a Cloud 60
If 10
I'll Tell You How the Sun Rose 61
In an Artist's Studio 145

Index of Titles

Invictus 101
Invitation to Love 148
'It is a beauteous evening, calm and free' 93
'It was a lover and his lass' 146

Jewish Prayer 50

L'amitié Est L'amour Sans Ailes 123
Leisure 7
'Lord, make me an instrument of Thy peace' 38
Love and Friendship 132
Love Lightly Pleased 147

Magna Est Veritas 81
May 74
May the Road Rise Up to Meet You 9
Meeting at Night 140
Miracles 39
Moonlight, Summer Moonlight 75
Moonlit Apples 84
My Heart Leaps Up 72
My Mind to Me a Kingdom Is 22

New Every Morning 99
New Friends and Old Friends 133
New Sights 5
No Coward Soul Is Mine 117
Now May Every Living Thing 12

Ode 92
On a Quiet Conscience 6
On First Looking into Chapman's Homer 24
Outwitted 126

Index of Titles

'Pack, clouds, away, and welcome day' 168
Pangur Bán 173
Pied Beauty 35
Pleasant Sounds 88

Rest and Be Thankful! 82
Rose-cheeked Laura 144

Say Not the Struggle Nought Availeth 97
Seal Lullaby 177
'See yonder leafless trees against the sky' 89
Shining Things 17
Shut Not Your Doors to Me, Proud Libraries 106
Song of Apollo 20
Song 154
Sonnet 18 139
Sowing 69
Spring 59
Swing Low, Sweet Chariot 46

Thanks in Old Age 30
The Argument of His Book 57
The Call 108
The Gettysburg Address 113
The Happy Child 62
The Iroquois Prayer 49
The Lake Isle of Innisfree 76
The Lurcher 162
The New Colossus 112
The Owl and the Pussycat 175
The Quiet Life 19
The Selkirk Grace 53
The Shape of a Good Greyhound 161
The Song of Wandering Aengus 58

Index of Titles

The Star-Spangled Banner   114
The Sun Rising   67
The Thanksgivings   42
The Throstle   73
The Windhover   165
This, Too, Shall Pass Away   104
To a Friend   141
To Althea, from Prison   155
To Autumn   86
To Every Thing There Is a Season   15
To Make a Prairie   78
Travelling   131

Upon Julia's Clothes   143

We Two Boys Together Clinging   127
When I Heard at the Close of the Day   153
When the Heart is Hard   52
Where the Bee Sucks   77
Will   100

Index of First Lines

A head like a snake 161
A little health 31
A thing of beauty is a joy for ever 16
All you *big* things, bless the Lord 41
Amazing grace, how sweet the sound 36
At the top of the house the apples are laid in rows 84

Busy old fool, unruly sun 67

Close thine eyes, and sleep secure 6
Come when the nights are bright with stars 148
Come, ye thankful people, come 44
Courage is the price that Life exacts for granting peace 107
Crisply the bright snow whispered 166

Doubling and doubling with laborious walk 82
Drop a pebble in the water: just a splash, and it is gone 109

Earth has not anything to show more fair 83
Every day is a fresh beginning 99

For ADORATION seasons change 66
For flowers that bloom about our feet 40
For I will consider my cat Jeoffry 169
Forth goes the woodman, leaving unconcerned 162
Four score and seven years ago our fathers brought forth on this continent 113
From our low seat beside the fire 108

Index of First Lines

Give me my scallop-shell of quiet 51
Give me the long, straight road before me 98
Glory be to God for dappled things 35
Go placidly amid the noise and haste 47
God be in my head 37
God give me work 54
Good morning, Life – and all 64

Had I the heavens' embroidered cloths 137
Hail to thee, blithe Spirit! 167
Happy the man, and happy he alone 4
Happy the man, whose wish and care 19
Hast thou named all the birds without a gun? 129
He drew a circle that shut me out 126
He who binds to himself a joy 25
Here, in this little Bay 81
'Hope' is the thing with feathers 105
How do I love thee? Let me count the ways 138
Hurt no living thing 13

I and Pangur Bán, my cat 173
I ask but one thing of you, only one 141
I caught this morning morning's minion, king- 165
I have lived and I have loved 119
I hear America singing, the varied carols I hear 116
I know a bank where the wild thyme blows 79
I like to see a thing I know 5
I love all shining things 17
I love to wander at my idle will 80
I planted a young tree when I was young 70
I saw Eternity the other night 27
I saw this day sweet flowers grow thick 62
I sing of brooks, of blossoms, birds, and bowers 57
I stood beside a hill 65

Index of First Lines

I thank all who have loved me in their hearts 151
I wandered lonely as a cloud 60
I went out to the hazel wood 58
I will arise and go now, and go to Innisfree 76
I'll tell you how the Sun rose 61
If you can keep your head when all about you 10
It is a beauteous evening, calm and free 93
It was a lover and his lass 146
It was a perfect day 69

Let fair or foul my mistress be 147
Like a quetzal plume, a fragrant flower 130
Lord, make me an instrument of Thy peace 38
Love is like the wild rose-briar 132

Make new friends, but keep the old 133
May the road rise up to meet you 9
Much have I travell'd in the realms of gold 24
My fairest child, I have no song to give you 26
My heart is like a singing bird 142
My heart leaps up when I behold 72
My mind to me a kingdom is 22

No coward soul is mine 117
Not like the brazen giant of Greek fame 112
Now may every living thing, young or old 12

O say, can you see, by the dawn's early light 114
O! the month of May, the merry month of May 74
Oh! hush thee, my baby, the night is behind us 177
Oh! I have slipped the surly bonds of Earth 8
Oh, the comfort 128
Once more the liberal year laughs out 85
One face looks out from all his canvases 145

Index of First Lines

Out of the night that covers me 101
Outside the sky is light with stars 152

Pack, clouds, away, and welcome day 168

Rose-cheeked Laura, come 144

Say not the struggle nought availeth 97
Season of mists and mellow fruitfulness! 86
See yonder leafless trees against the sky 89
Shall I compare thee to a summer's day? 139
Shut not your doors to me, proud libraries 106
Some have meat and cannot eat 53
Sound the Flute! 59
Summer is coming, summer is coming 73
Swing low, sweet chariot 46

Thanks in old age – thanks ere I go 30
That man over there say 102
The Day's grown old, the fainting Sun 90
The grey sea and the long black land 140
The Owl and the Pussy-cat went to sea 175
The rustling of leaves under the feet in woods and under hedges 88
The sleepless Hours who watch me as I lie 20
The spacious firmament on high 92
The world is charged with the grandeur of God 94
The world is so full 3
The year's at the spring 63
There is no chance, no destiny, no fate 100
There is no happier life 150
This day is called the feast of Crispian 111
This is the spot: – how mildly does the sun 131
Thou that hast giv'n so much to me 28

Index of First Lines

Though our mouths were full of song as the sea 50
'Tis moonlight, summer moonlight 75
To every thing there is a season 15
To make a prairie it takes a clover and one bee 78
To see a World in a Grain of Sand 14

We return thanks to our mother, the earth, which sustains us 49
We two boys together clinging 127
We who are here present thank the Great Spirit that we are here to praise Him 42
What is this life if, full of care 7
When as in silks my Julia goes 143
When as the rye reach to the chin 154
When I heard at the close of the day how my name had been receiv'd with plaudits in the capitol, still it was not a happy night for me that follow'd 153
When Love with unconfinèd wings 155
When some great sorrow like a mighty river 104
When the heart is hard and parched up, come upon me with a shower of mercy 52
When you came, you were like red wine and honey 157
Where the bee sucks, there suck I 77
Why should my anxious breast repine 123
Why, who makes much of a miracle? 39
With thee conversing I forget all time 149

You little friend, your nose is ready; you sniff 163

MACMILLAN COLLECTOR'S LIBRARY

Own the world's great works of literature in one beautiful collectible library

Designed and curated to appeal to book lovers everywhere, Macmillan Collector's Library editions are small enough to travel with you and striking enough to take pride of place on your bookshelf. These much-loved literary classics also make the perfect gift.

Beautifully made, every Macmillan Collector's Library book adheres to the same high production values. Each hardback features gilt edges, a ribbon marker and cloth binding, and every paperback has a bespoke illustrated cover.

Discover a new and exciting anthology or cherish your favourite classic stories with this elegant collection.

Macmillan Collector's Library: own, collect, and treasure

Discover the full range at
panmacmillan.com/mcl